W9-AVL-176

Praise for *Throwing The Elephant*

". . . smartly funny. Bing has mortared his bricks of humor with undeniable truths."
—*Boston Globe*

"Read this and you, too, can deal with the boss."
—*USA Today*

"It's Mel Brooks meets the Bodhisattva."
—*Business Week*

"The elephant in question is the boss himself and Mr. Bing provides charmingly cynical advice. The nuggets within are golden."
—*Wall Street Journal*

"Wickedly funny."
—*Dallas Morning News*

Stanley Bing is a columnist for *Fortune* magazine and the author of the national bestseller *What Would Machiavelli Do?*, and the novels *Lloyd: What Happened* and *You Look Nice Today*. By day, he works for a gigantic multinational conglomerate whose identity is one of the worst-kept secrets in business.

Throwing the Elephant

ZEN AND THE ART OF MANAGING UP

Stanley Bing

HarperBusiness
An Imprint of HarperCollins*Publishers*

THROWING THE ELEPHANT. Copyright © 2002 by Stanley Bing. All rights reserved. Printed in the United States of America. No part of this book may be used or reproduced in any manner whatsoever without written permission except in the case of brief quotations embodied in critical articles and reviews. For information address HarperCollins Publishers Inc., 10 East 53rd Street, New York, NY 10022.

HarperCollins books may be purchased for educational, business, or sales promotional use. For information please write: Special Markets Department, HarperCollins Publishers Inc., 10 East 53rd Street, New York, NY 10022.

First HarperBusiness paperback edition published 2003

Designed by Nicola Ferguson

The Library of Congress has catalogued the hardcover edition as follows:

Bing, Stanley.
    Throwing the elephant : Zen and the art of managing up /
by Stanley Bing.—1st ed.
        p. cm.
    ISBN 0-06-018861-8
    1. Managing your boss. 2. Interpersonal relations—Religious aspects—Buddhism. 3. Zen Buddhism. I. Title.

HF5548.83 .B563 2002
650.1'3—dc21

2001039801

ISBN 0-06-093422-0 (pbk.)

03   04   05 06 07 /QM/ 10   9   8   7   6   5   4   3   2   1

ACKNOWLEDGMENTS

To all the elephants in my corporation
both very great and small
and to the littlest elephant of them all,
my editor, David Hirshey

And to my wife, as always

Who has no-thought? Who is not-born?
If we are truly not-born,
We are not un-born either . . .
Release your hold on earth, water, fire, wind;
Drink and eat as you wish in eternal serenity;
All things are transient and completely empty,
This is the great enlightenment.

ANCIENT JAPANESE SUTRA

Make me one with everything.

ZEN MASTER
ORDERING A HOT DOG

CONTENTS

What This Book Is About

> You gotta serve somebody.
> *BOB DYLAN*

I had a boss one time who said a wise thing to me. This isn't a pedestrian occurrence in the daily run of things, so I paid attention.

"You can't choose your boss," he said to me.

This idea was expressed with some sadness. He was a President. I was not. But the feeling was something we shared from our relative positions in the cosmos of the Corporation.

I have thought of that statement many times in the years since that boss, whom I did not choose, went off to play golf for the rest of his life. And the more I think of it, the more true it seems.

You can't choose your boss.

Go to the shelf of the gargantuan supermarket of ideas and no-ideas that is your local bookseller and stop in front of the Business section, which for reasons that are beyond me is usually far, far away from Philosophy and way too close to Computing.

You will see there dozens and dozens of books purporting to help the scared, scarred, leery, angry, hopeful, ambitious, hopeless, confused, frustrated, demented employee determine some strategy for dealing with the person they have been assigned to serve.

We need not go into the variety of nonsense that is suggested to people. All of it is based on the idea that power can be managed through rational means.

It can't.

To get a handle on the problem, one must walk away from Business, in which, sadly, you have probably found this book . . . and walk over to the grandfather of Philosophy: Religion.

For it is only through a leap of faith that one may gain one's footing in the tumultuous, slippery terrain in which unruly, unreasoning, selfish, mean, crafty, manipulative, infantile, and belligerent power can be managed and ultimately, yes, controlled.

It can be done!

But not by you. Not as you are now. You need Brahma on your side. Or at least something that brings you close to Brahma.

Now, many fine religions tend to the human soul. They have their place, each and all. Some provide better food on holidays, but all have their happy adherents and it is bootless to get into which might be better than the other. Whatever you are born to, you should probably stick to it.

But one thing is certain. Only the power of Zen contemplation will result in a happy business life for the subordinate who yearns for understanding, control, and enlightenment. Best of all, Zen works in total coordination with all other established religions, so you can keep yours while you work. That's convenient.

Zen taps our internal reservoir of peace that surpasses all understanding.

Zen can be done sitting down, while staring off into space. Don't you do a lot of that already?

Zen removes us from the foolishness of everyday life and give us the perspective to go on when every fiber of our being is screaming for release.

Zen changes the ground on which you stand, the perspective from which you see things, enabling you to rise above and beyond the passions and griefs that attend service to the elephant that lives in the corner office.

Zen will enable you to take an object of enormous weight and size and mold it in your grasp like a ball of Silly Putty. For senior management is, in truth, the silliest putty of them all.

If you are patient, trusting, and disciplined, Zen will enable you to lift that enormous object over your head and heave it as Chuck Norris would hoist a bad guy ten times his size into the mirror behind the bar.

And it is the practice of Business Zen that will enable you, in the end, after much trial and failure, to throw the elephant who is your boss.

On Elephants, and How They Are Different from People

Heinrich von Pierer, the sixty-year-old chief executive officer of Germany's Siemens AG, is so fierce on the tennis court that such prominent opponents as German chancellor Gerhard Schroeder have given up trying to beat him. One story goes like this: During a game of doubles, the trim Mr. von Pierer was teamed up with a portly partner against Mr. Schroeder and another player. Frustrated at having fallen behind, Mr. von Pierer yelled at his teammate: "You have to hate your opponent!" before instructing him to simply stand still in a corner. Then Mr. von Pierer dashed back and forth across the court in a one-man show to take the set.

WALL STREET JOURNAL
FEBRUARY 2, 2001

Once upon a time, a blind man was assigned by the corporation to handle a very large and difficult elephant.

First he felt around the front of the elephant with his hands. There seemed to be a gigantic, smiling opening with a serpentine protrusion coming out of the front. To the side of the creature, he encountered a vast wall of leather that at certain points hardened to the consistency of stone. In the back, two large, wrinkled, globular objects were positioned around a moist central region. What was he to infer from this area?

Later, he met with his senior manager. "Well," said the bodhisattva who oversaw his spiritual development, "tell me how you would describe the beast that you just had the opportunity of encountering."

"It was equally inscrutable all the way around," said the blind man. He was immediately seized by the guards, who hauled him roughly to the basement and threw him with no ceremony into a large pond teeming with crocodiles. "What did I do to deserve this?" he cried as the vicious reptiles tore his flesh from its underpinning of bone.

"Are you kidding?" said his supervisor. "Anyone who can't tell the front of the elephant from the back of the elephant deserves whatever he gets."

I'm afraid we felt the wrong end of the elephant first.

ALAN WAGNER, VP, CBS, ON
THE FAILURE OF THE NIGHTTIME DRAMA,
BEACON HILL, 1975

Many animals walk the earth. Only some of them are elephants. The rest of us must deal with them.

Some of us are gnus, and this is unfortunate unless one chooses the path of the gnu, and then there is certainly nothing wrong with it. There is a place in the universe for bovine creatures of various sizes who eat vegetables at lunchtime and do no violence to anyone. Good luck to them!

Others are lions, but it is a well-known fact that lions do not prevail over the average elephant. Lions are fierce and noble, but they too may be crushed under the elephantine foot. One may also be a little bird pecking away the insects that prey upon the elephant's hide. But what kind of living is that?

> *When you have got an elephant*
> *by the hind leg,*
> *and he is trying to run away,*
> *it's best to let him run.*
> ABRAHAM LINCOLN

No, the way of dignity is first to recognize that one is not an elephant, and then to dedicate one's life to serving and controlling these gigantic and powerful beasts.

It is possible. Their size is illusory. Their power is evanescent. They will all go to the elephant graveyard, eventually. In the meantime, they need our help.

ELEPHANT FACTS

- The elephant weighs a great deal. Many ordinary people weigh a lot, but none weighs as much as an elephant. Even when elephants are thin and desiccated, they are very, very heavy.
- Elephants are also tall, even when they are short. Even a short elephant is taller than a normal person.
- Elephants eat a tremendous amount, tons and tons of food every week, even though for many of

them it is mostly tuna and salad. No matter how much or how well a normal human being can eat, there is no way he or she can eat as much as an elephant.

- Elephants are hedonistic, even in their self-denial.

- Elephants are accustomed to getting what they want. When they don't, they make a lot of noise and threaten the well-being of their handlers and fellow elephants.

- Elephants play by rules of their own devising. These rules often make no sense to anyone but the elephant, and there is no inherent reason to follow them other than that the elephant will hurt you if you do not.

- Elephants exult in their size and power. As it is written (in the *Wall Street Journal*), Sanford Weill, the chairman of Citigroup, dressed up as Moses before an audience of retainers and sycophants to celebrate the defeat of his rival, John Reed, for control of the Company back in the late 1990s. This elephant's sense of propriety was so great that he gave not one on-the-record quote in a laudatory profile in the Sunday *New York Times Magazine*. And yet, in his victory over what he perceived to be the forces of Pharaoh, he might be seen in long beard and gown exulting over the demise of his enemies. The audience was convulsed with laughter, since nothing is quite as amusing as an elephant in a playful mood.

- Elephants have short attention spans. Many have been known to fire and rehire people on the same day. As we move along the path, we will develop the ability to discount elephant displays of emotion by more than 90 percent. This is a good discount and should be taken advantage of by anybody who is offered it.

- Elephants are clean and fastidious animals by nature. They like to dress well and travel in conveyances designed with their needs in mind. They become angry and quite dangerous if their transportation does not arrive on time and they are forced to stand around doing nothing.

- Elephants hate doing nothing unless they can call it a meeting.

- To a real elephant, and not a sheep, wolf, or gnu in elephant's clothing, you are not there. There is no You. There is no Is. There is only the Elephant. Don't you see how silly that is? And how silly it makes the elephant? Ha ha ha on the elephant!

- Elephants are terrific bullshit artists and are never doing quite as well as you think they are. This audacity makes them great, if slightly smelly.

- The elephant cannot be ignored. It must be understood and directed this way and that. It can be done, because for some strange reason, in spite of all their size and power, elephants need direction and know it.

- Most important of all—elephants cannot be anything but elephants. No matter what pressure they are under, they do not become rats or mice, they do not revert to human form. They remain elephants. And you are not one of them. In that lies your pathway to salvation and upward management.

Upward management! It is the way and the light to those who labor in darkness. Through the Four (or possibly Five) Truths and the Ninefold Path shall you know and come to live it. It is the way of Biz Zen.

BIZ ZEN: WHAT IS IT?

Zen is many things, many solutions to many mysteries. But in its heart, it is this: the knowledge of the universe and all its workings that comes from sitting.

That's right. Sitting. Year after year of sitting in the position of thought and comfort (sometimes in a very nice leather recliner), and by working without hope of spiritual (not to mention financial) recompense, reaching for the lightness of being that comes with the renunciation of hope and desire.

In this way, by sitting and sitting and sitting until everything suddenly becomes lighter, you can achieve enlightenment and through enlightenment—power.

And happiness. For, yes, such as we may be happier than any elephant can ever be. Yes, it is easier for a camel to fit through the eye of a needle than for an elephant to achieve happiness. The average middle manager wolfing down a hot dog at a sideboard provided for his use has an easier time of it. Because elephants are driven by desire. And desire is misery.

In the end, the elephant—your elephant—will and can always be nothing more nor less than itself. This is its greatest strength and its greatest weakness.

You, on the other hand, can be anything you want. Because you are too small to be entitled to a self. And that is your greatest pathway to peace and enlighten-ment. For the self is bondage.

Get over yourself! How good does that feel!

Your elephant cannot get over its self. And it lives on and on with that gigantic, gray self . . . until, inevitably, it does not. And then? There is a new elephant. There will always be a new elephant.

And that new elephant will be nothing more nor less, once again, than itself.

But you? You can be anything! Because your self—it is nothing! Good for you.

It is up to others to make what they can of the ele-phant, its size, its weight, its intransigent nature. Those who can do so may eradicate the inevitable suffering of life.

Those who do not will be swept along with the tide.

Buddha in Business

Anything that you can do without a great deal of thought
becomes a perfect form of meditation, whether it's shuck-
ing peas, digging up a plot of ground, putting up a fence, or
doing dishes.

ZEN MASTER ALAN WATTS

Conquer the self, and you will conquer the opponent.

TAKUAN SOHO

If you're going to be thinking, you might as well think big.

DONALD TRUMP

THE STORY OF THE BUDDHA

A very long time ago, or not, there lived a young man
in the suburbs of a very great city, or perhaps it was
not a great city. It could have been Bridgeport. Does it
matter?

Young Sid Arthur was a part of a great family, a family of rich and powerful businessmen who ruled their
metropolitan area in the days before consolidation.

By the time Arthur attained enlightenment, he had

grown quite fat and also bald, with the big, round tummy and smiling face and eyes we have come to associate with his Buddha status. But in his youth Arthur was good-looking with a big head of unruly hair and was also popular among both men and women as quite the party animal. He was always the guy who refused to go home at 3 A.M. when the rest of the pack was ready to head back to the hotel; always the one who could conceive of one more cocktail when the rest were contemplating the possibility of going facedown in the onion dip.

His father raised the young man to be a scion of the ruling class. He went to Andover, then Yale, and from thence to the Wharton School of Business.

He was a happy lad, and while he excelled in all his studies, he also played squash and poker with distinction.

It became clear quite early in his business career, however, that there was something different about the young man. When the Steinbergs, Perelmans, and other Wharonites would upon graduation go out hunting for small companies to destabilize and acquire, the future Buddha would hang back, disgusted.

It is told that, on one occasion, his associates targeted and successfully brought down a small telecommunications concern, preparing to merge it into one of the larger wireless carriers that was then looking to purchase revenue growth, being unable to generate it internally.

Just as the little company was falling to earth and the brokers were descending upon it, drooling for their fat transaction fees, the young man stepped in and established excellent exit packages for existing senior management and even managed to save a good portion of middle management from the transitional ax.

The brokers were greatly angered, for they were

determined to reduce headcount cheaply. But the boy's father saw that something special in his son that might incapacitate him for serious business work. So he kept a keen eye on his son from then on, sequestering him in the family business and allowing him to take a lot of nice vacations and long business trips to Ritz-Carltons around the world.

During that time, the young man met and married a beautiful young woman who had completed her law degree from Columbia University but had decided to pursue her MBA afterward because she had no desire to practice law. Who does? Still, they were happy.

Everything was thus going along pretty much as expected for the youthful Buddha. He never left the general environs of his office, his home, and the series of hotels at which the privileged business traveler can park himself between meetings.

Then one day he was invited to spend an extended period of time within the confines of another corporation with whom his people were working out some kind of joint venture.

While in their conference room perusing some papers, he came upon a middle manager who was being yelled at by a senior vice president of finance. The poor man's shoulders were bent with anguish, his eyes were red and runny with sadness and humiliation, his hands shook, and he could scarcely raise his voice to defend himself.

"What is this?" our young hero asked an associate. "Why does that man scream at the other man? And why is the other content to suffer such indignities?"

"It is thus everywhere, my friend," said his associate, a fellow named Beebe, who, incidentally, stayed with him until the end of his life. "That is the way of management from time immemorial, in medieval feudal states, communist dictatorships, and capitalist conference rooms alike. It is the way the powerful treat those less so, and it is the human condition."

"You don't say," said the Buddha. And he became very thoughtful indeed.

Later on in the afternoon, he came to a small office not far from the rest rooms, where a rather elderly man in an old-fashioned three-piece suit was sitting at a desk cutting up paper dolls. "Why does that perfectly good person sit and waste his time like that?" the Buddha asked his associate.

"That too is the way of things," said Beebe. "He has mismanaged himself at the height of his career and is now destined to endure day to day with great suffering and uselessness because his senior management doesn't know how to utilize him."

"Ah," said the Buddha, troubled at heart. It was clear to him that each of these individuals he had seen was doomed to live in intense suffering that defined his existence, simply because he or she could not manage the elephant.

In the days and months that followed, his eyes now open, the budding Buddha beheld the pain and suffering that is the inexorable fate of people who work for elephants. "Is there nothing I can do to ease the hurt that lies at the heart of working existence?" he asked himself over and over.

And so, in his thirtieth year, Sid Arthur determined to drop out of corporate life and go as a consultant from place to place begging for retainers in an attempt to come face-to-face with as much management-created suffering as he possibly could, hoping that in this search for understanding he might eventually determine a way to eradicate the pain that lies at the nature of business employment.

BUDDHA
THE LEAN (BUT NOT MEAN) YEARS

For the next seven years, the master wandered from corporation to corporation, looking for answers.

First, he studied with a group of ascetics devoted to the notion of Quality, in which, they believed, constant attention to process and the wishes of the customer placed one on the pathway to freedom and happiness.

The future Buddha mastered the Quality Process, but found that it did little to bring happiness to any but a very few tyrannical maniacs at the top of the heap. This felt too much like business as usual, and he moved on.

Next he found a group of mendicants who were obsessed with the production of shareholder value. For a time, he thought perhaps that through this total purity of spirit, some truth could be found. But nowhere in his experience did he actually find more intense confusion and suffering among working people below the rank of chairman. No depredation visited on employees large and small was considered too rank and cruel if it made even one security analyst enthusiastic for an afternoon. The master moved on.

Visiting both coasts, he studied for a time under those who labored within cults of personality. In this way, he walked quietly within the halls of Diller and Welch, Eisner and Gerstner, Gates and Ellison and Enrico, and found that happiness was possible there, but in the end too fragile to be maintained.

Over and over, young Arthur came face-to-face with the underlying truth of all who work: that to labor is to suffer, and probably for too little money.

He realized a new answer must be found to solve the problem of human suffering.

As he went forth, the master considered all varieties of self-denial to reach the goal he sought. At first, he allowed himself no expense account activity whatsoever, believing that in the absence of pleasure lay the way of wisdom. He ate neither granola at breakfast nor Cobb salad at noon and at dinnertime took in perhaps a cheeseburger in a local diner or a slice of pizza at a roadside stand, nothing more.

This yielded nothing but indigestion.

At last he determined that in expense account deprivation lay a sense of denied entitlement that distracted the seeker from the object of his quest. After that, he ate and drank much like a normal business professional and would by no means fly first class unless business class was fully booked.

And still he sought until he could stand seeking no longer, looking for the key that would unlock all suffering, at least between the hours of eight in the morning and seven in the evening, except on the West Coast, where they knock off earlier.

And then there came a day when he could stand the quest no longer, and he said to himself, "Oh, the heck with it."

And thus in his thirty-seventh year, he went off on his own into the desert just outside Palm Springs, which is very hot but certainly very comfortable, because it is dry heat and you practically can't feel it like you can in more humid climes where you sweat through your clothing almost immediately. There in the desert he explored new forms of meditation, forms that were congenial to Business, for in truth it is easier to meditate and thus reach enlightenment when you have nothing to do and your Palm is not receiving a clear signal.

And then one morning, with his heart heavy within him, he took a cigar out into the desert, since it is impossible to find a place where you can smoke indoors nowadays, and he sat underneath a tree and decided he would reconcile himself to the fact that being managed by other people is pain, and there is nothing for it but to quit or learn to manage the unmanageable.

After finishing his cigar, the Buddha fell into a trance, or a coma of some kind, one that allowed him to continue sitting up, anyway.

Afternoon became night and night turned into day and still he did not move.

When he arose the next morning, stiff in his limbs but infinitely light in spirit, he was no longer the business professional who had sat down the day before. The power born of enlightenment radiated from him, and with it the ability to free other men and women from their suffering.

For a time, Buddha considered just chucking the whole thing and taking off for Saint Bart's. He was feeling pretty good and didn't have any great confidence that the lesson he was about to teach would be embraced by miserable people mired in their lusts for power and money.

But he considered. If he did not pass along his wisdom, what had the search been all about?

So he met with several friends who had planned to golf with him that day and made them sit down and explained to them the truth that had finally shone upon him. And they listened and were moved and changed forever, then themselves went out to teach the new wisdom after getting in nine holes later in the afternoon.

For the next forty-five years, Buddha wandered from place to place, never picking up a check unless it was absolutely necessary. Everywhere he went, he taught the same simple truth, the essence of which may perhaps best be stated in the text of what Buddha said in his first discussion with his disciples at the Doubletree in Dallas. As it is said:

> There is no suffering for him who has completed his journey, who is freed from sorrow, who has freed himself on all sides, who has shaken off all fetters.
>
> *THE DHAMMAPADA*

No fetters! What a concept. Let's begin to shake them off right now with some helpful wisdom in a form that any business student will recognize, take comfort from, and be able to understand.

BUDDHA BULLETS

GETTING STARTED

◌ We are all one with the corporation. It has no beginning and no end. So relax. Nothing really matters all that much.

‣ We are all incomprehensibly tiny in the eye of the infinite. That includes the gigantic elephant who right now is sitting on your head.

‣ Truly, there is no "we," no "me," no "I." There is only the universe that is the corporation. You are part of it and it is part of you. It has no beginning and no end, and neither do you. You are everything and everything is you.

‣ There is large. There is no small. There is only the corporation.

‣ The heaviest of entities within the body of the corporation has no weight, the lightest is as heavy as the greatest. Anything else is simply an illusion in an expensive suit.

‣ There is no past. There is no future. There is only now. And in the now there is simply Duty, the thing to be done, and nothing else.

‣ The corporation goes on. If we are part of the corporation, it goes on. If we are not part of the corporation, it goes on. If we are happy, it goes on. If we are not, it goes on. Nothing matters, because everything will go on whether it matters or does not matter, because it is in the nature of things that they should go on. There is no meaning in it. There is just the going on.

‣ There is no forward and no backward. So stop trying to get ahead.

‣ It is the wanting of things that makes us suffer. In the

lack of wanting, there is joy. In the end of hope and desire, there is Enlightenment.

○ So: There is no boss. There is no reporting structure. All that is an illusion. There is only the work and the beautiful serenity of the eternal whole. Get with it! It is you!

Throwing the Elephant

Personal Preparation

THE FOUR OR FIVE TRUTHS

THE NINEFOLD PATH

ENLIGHTENING UP!

The incomparable lion-roar of the doctrine
Shatters the brains of the one hundred kinds of animals.
Even the king of elephants will run away, forgetting his pride;
Only the heavenly dragon listens calmly, with pure delight.

ZEN TEXT

You only get what you are big enough to take.

JIMMY HOFFA JR.

The ways to find one's way to Enlightenment are many. There is prayer and fasting, and some try that to great effect, but that road is severe, particularly to people with electronic scheduling software and a lot of business lunches as part of the general requirements of their jobs, not to mention drinks after work, and pretty soon fasting, if not prayer, is out the window.

The Buddha was quite clear on this subject: if Enlightenment was reserved for those who don't have to work for a living, it would be a pretty unfair deal all the way around.

The Buddha said it, and the scriptures make it clear over and over. In work lies Enlightenment just as surely as in wandering around in a bathrobe with a bowl of rice in one hand and a stick in the other. One need not

3

remove oneself from the world to transcend it. One must use the tools that are put in one's path. Perhaps a tale might elucidate this point.

One morning the Buddha stopped by a barbershop for a little touch-up. The barber was a voluble and philosophical fellow, as many of that profession tend to be, and he regaled the Buddha with a host of meaningless anecdotes and flippant observations in which the Buddha had no interest.

At the end of an especially broad and runny river of drivel, Buddha closed his eyes and took one of those deep, cleansing breaths that afterward became such an important part of his teaching. The barber at last noticed this and set down his scissors thoughtfully.

"Oh, Buddha," he said into the gigantic void that was parked, sighing profoundly, in the chair. "I notice that I have been speaking without stop for well unto twenty minutes and you have said not a word. Is there something you wish me to infer from this?"

The Buddha smiled, and the Buddha's smile was indeed a beautiful thing to see, shedding radiance all over the place. "Yes, my friend," the Buddha said. "Your job is to cut my hair. My job is to sit and have it cut. You see how close to perfection we might be if we each accomplished our duty without distractions."

The barber was immediately struck by the truth of this and miraculously said not a word for the rest of the haircut. Buddha got to read the new issue of *Car & Driver* and left a nice tip.

You see? That's how it works. Everybody does what he or she is supposed to do without a lot of fuss and noise and emotion. Things get lighter. The lighter they get, the more enlightened you become. Pretty soon, nothing makes any particular difference. Except the work.

> *In the tree, the nightingale sings;*
> *What else should he do?*
> *It takes but three*
> *To line the cooking pot!*
>
> Bo Ho
> A.D. 342

A steelworker makes steel, and in that action lies his Enlightenment. An accountant loses himself in his rows of numbers and may thus find the pathway to his oneness with the Universe. For others, the road to wisdom lies in two frequent states of being: sitting and silence. Mostly in meetings.

Sitting. And silence. Both are at the heart of Zen. They are also at the heart of the work we do.

Think about it. We are in a meeting. We sit. We are silent. At times, true, there is a verbal duty for us to perform, so we speak. And then, others speak. And while they speak? We are silent.

On our way to work, we sit on the train or in our car or we stand staring into the near middle distance like a cow in the field. We are going from here to there. What are we doing? Nothing. In that nothing lies everything.

We receive our mail, both electronic and paper, throughout the day. While we evaluate and respond to it, we sit. We are silent. At times, true, others enter our domain and require speech or reaction from us, but when they are gone, we return to our task and while we do so? We sit. And are silent.

We sit on a transcontinental airliner, traveling for four or five hours for a meeting whose meat will occupy perhaps ten or fifteen minutes. We stare out the window of the plane, trying to decide whether to watch the in-flight entertainment. We sit and are silent.

Between planes, we watch the inescapable CNN feed on the television that is bolted to the ceiling. A portion of our minds is taken up with the interesting story of the dancing bear that was adopted by a family of Bosnian dwarfs. But inside, as we sit with less than 10 percent of ourselves engaged, somewhere within, we are silent.

In that silence, there is liberation. There is peace. There is an end of desire, passion, and suffering.

We read papers that will shape our destiny. The *Wall Street Journal* thinks our industry is spiraling down into the toilet.

Our spirits rebel at what we read, be it newspaper, memo, or E-mail. Inside, we are a riot of feeling. But stop. Look within. Is there not something in there that really doesn't give a shit? Of course there is. In that place, there is silence. There is the Buddha.

There is the answer to the management and control of elephants both large and small.

Why, look. Here comes one now into our little corner of the village. "Owoooo!" It raises its trunk heavenward and lets out a trumpeting cry. Perhaps it dances around the area, crushing huts, villagers, and other things beneath its big, leathery feet. True, some run around the elephant, screaming, attempting to control it, move it this way or that. But not we. We sit. We are silent. Perhaps the elephant requires something of us by way of duty. Of course, then we accomplish that duty. Then we return to sit in silence again. The elephant has gone away! And then?

We sit. We are silent. And as water fills a well if we but allow it, we are filled with freedom and power.

Where does one get such access to peace and joy?

It begins, as the Buddha did, with a full understanding of the Four (or Five) Truths that lay the foundation for all future handling, managing, leveraging, and eventual hoisting and lifting of elephants both large and small.

THE FOUR (OR FIVE) TRUTHS

TRUTH #1: Work is suffering. The ability to boss other people around destroys much of human decency. Evidence suggests that even Gandhi was a jerk to work for, and he had quite a good image otherwise. There is no way to get around it. Bosses suck. Get over it.

TRUTH #2: Desire is the root of suffering. It is the desire to achieve, to live, to make things tolerable and pleasant, and even better, that creates untold pain in the lives of men and women. Want nothing, and you shall not be disappointed.

TRUTH #3: Suffering can be conquered. The self is the root of desire. One must eradicate the self to achieve peace that surpasses understanding. Only through Zen can the no-self transcend the power of others, liberate the soul, and win valuable prizes.

TRUTH #4: There is a path to end your suffering. We will embark on it now. It is a ninefold path that has nine steps in it, as all ninefold paths will, for the most part, except in Zen text, where sometimes they have ten.

TRUTH #5: There is no truth #5.

THE NINEFOLD PATH

The way of the martial artist is the way of enduring, sur-
viving, and prevailing over all that would destroy him.
The skill of the ninja is the art of winning.

TAKAMATSU TOSHITSUGU

A true pacifist is able to kill or maim in the blink of an
eye, but at the moment of impending destruction of the
enemy he chooses nonviolence.

YUKIYOSHI TAKAMURA

As a person who understood the world and its workings, Buddha knew that a vague and general approach
would not serve the majority of businesspeople as they
went about their duties while at the same time searching
for both enlightenment and a way to manage elephants.

He realized that there is no difference between those
two goals: managing elephants is a form of enlightenment, and enlightenment leads to the ability to lift, play
with, and throw even the heaviest of elephants.

But Buddha was not just a metaphysical fellow, he was
also well tooled in the ways of life on the road, and he
knew that businesspeople do not succeed by willpower
alone, that we need to-do lists to get our arms around
things.

At the very moment he was enjoying his first flush of enlightenment, Buddha happened by a newsstand. He wasn't looking for one, he was just wandering around basking in the glow of his new selfless status, enjoying the sensation of having come up with a really good idea, of being perched on the brink of the cosmos and otherwise feeling no pain. So for no particular reason, since nothing had any particular reason anymore, Buddha went into this upscale newsstand outside of Palm Springs in a little strip mall to get a pack of gum. "One may chew completely and therein achieve in that act a form of perfection," Buddha said to himself, but really he just wanted a pack of gum and that was reason enough for getting one. If he hadn't gotten one, it would have been all right, because he had flushed all desire from his system, but all things being equal he didn't mind having some gum and here was a newsstand right in front of him and so he went in.

As he chewed his gum with perfect attention, Buddha let his eye wander over the magazines that occupied an entire wall of the store. There, no matter the subject matter of each individual magazine, he saw numbers.

Numbers upon numbers and still more numbers.

"154 Ways to Flatten Your Tummy!"

"The Top 500 Corporations!"

"265 Ways to Please Your Man!"

"The 100 Best Investments!"

And so it went on. And the light shone upon Buddha and he understood that for common people to understand things, they need a numbered pathway to guide them. So he came up with one.

The Ninefold Path

◇ *NOT CARING:* To get where you are going, you have to come from the right place. The first step is to wake up and smell the coffee, to step off the common path and head off into the trees. This is not an easy, shallow thing, but until one develops the ability to not care one bit about anything, one is at the mercy of the forces that act upon us.

◇ *NOT HOPING:* Things aren't going to get better, and even if they did on, say, Tuesday, by Wednesday they would most likely be worse again, and if not Wednesday, Thursday.

◇ *NOT SPEAKING:* How much wind we all expel and how little we say! Let the elephant do the noise-making. Tend toward silence. It enables us to abstain from lying, slander, abuse, and excessive self-promotion. And when you do speak, make it count. A picture is worth a thousand words. Silence is golden. A stitch in time saves nine. Hello!

◇ *NOT REACTING:* No-talking the no-talk is only half the battle. No-walking the no-walk is the other. In the face of elephant excess, show very little, and what you do show, don't.

◇ *NOT JUDGING:* Everyone else may do the wrong thing, but there's nothing wrong with that as long as they don't hurt anybody. True, they hurt everybody a lot of the time, but still, who are you to accuse anybody? Knock it off!

◇ *NOT LISTENING:* This is quite different than not hearing. Not hearing is bad. You must try to hear everything. But listen to nothing except direct orders and, if you have one in your office, television.

◇ **NOT THINKING:** Cogitation without thought is the goal. Clear your mind. Keep it that way. The Buddha knew a programming executive in Los Angeles several years ago who only used thoughts from other people and generated none himself. He did very well. Then one day he got big enough to start thinking on his own. He was gone in two months. Consider that, without really thinking about it, if you will.

◇ **NOT FEELING:** Our feelings for the elephant are the greatest obstacle to its management, and the most destructive emotion of all is fear. One cannot lift and throw an object of which one is afraid. You must lose your fear. The first step is doing away with all feelings for the elephant whatsoever, except perhaps for the overriding feelings of love that we as Zen practitioners must have for all dumb creatures of the universe, even the dangerous ones.

◇ **NOT PLANNING:** Keep the mind's eye focused on the *now*. The future is an illusion, particularly in merged companies. Instead of planning, sit and meditate on your blotter. Let your mind wander. Pretty soon you will be not planning with the best of them!

◇ **NOT GIVING UP:** What's the point? But seriously. Many is the person who gives up, only to find he could instead have been forced out with a great parachute. In the end, giving up is a form of egotism. Your job is to do your job. Keep going!

Together, these nine steps, achieved in silence, sitting, and contemplation, will deliver the proper attitude and understanding—if you are of light enough heart to receive it. So lighten up, for God's sake!

ENLIGHTENING UP!

As soon as one craves anything, one is plundered by outside
objects. When you indulge in likes and desires, then an
avaricious mind arises. When you like getting offerings,
then thoughts of striving and contention arise. If you like
obedient followers, then petty flatterers will join you. If
you like to score victories, then there is a gigantic rift
between yourself and others. If you like to exploit people,
then voices of resentment will be heard. . . . If the mind is
not aroused, myriad spontaneous things disappear.

ENGRAVED ON A STONE AT NANNING

Life sucks, and then you die.

ANONYMOUS

Several years ago, a group of Westinghouse executives
were sitting around a table at the Four Seasons Hotel in
Los Angeles, meeting about a subject the exact nature of
which is now lost in the mists of time. There is, after all,
no more Westinghouse, so of what importance could
the subject of their meeting have been?

An employee of the hotel entered the room and
informed the group that a large band of angry local citi-
zens was even then entering the neighborhood of the
hotel with less than good intentions.

Riots had erupted throughout the city. People were

firing at airplanes attempting to leave the local airport. Cars were being burned. It was most definitely time to go.

The Buddha was sitting at the meeting contemplating the inevitability of suffering, particularly his own, and was startled to hear the news.

"We should leave now and attempt to locate an area of greater safety," he said to his associates, many of whom were at that moment continuing to assemble large platefuls of cold cuts.

The meeting over, two monks approached the Buddha, who was preparing to achieve some higher ground almost immediately. "Say, Buddha," said the older one. "We were thinking of trying to get in nine holes at Bel Air before things got too bad. Want to come?"

The Buddha declined, with an admiring smile: "No, my friends. There are other places I must be."

So the Buddha, instead of indulging in such frivolity in the midst of crisis, went, it is said, to the roof of the hotel, where there was a swimming pool and where a very nice fruit plate was served him.

From that vantage point he watched the progress of the civil unrest with a large group that included Harvey Keitel, always one of the Buddha's favorites, and several tanned agents from the William Morris Agency, who spent the whole time on the telephone.

How does one achieve such a state of perpetual grace? Relaxation, that is how. Relaxation so profound it can weather any conflagration. Relaxation that is achieved through meditation, meditation that focuses our minds down to a tiny point in which there is no room for self, for desire, for passion.

Jack Welch plays golf, or else. Martha Stewart knows how to prepare and enjoy a cocktail when she's not contemplating the perfect wreath, and she does both with equal excellence. Donald Trump bags German supermodels and puts his name on anything that isn't nailed down, and even some things that are.

Each of these great elephants has discovered the elemental truth of enlightenment and happiness: things are never so serious that you can't take things light.

And yet we who are small, how serious are we! We rush around like demented ferrets while those who run the universe float by in big Town Cars with minibars!

The key to the ultimate release from seriousness is meditation. Meditation, at least for beginners, is simply the act of sitting and thinking until one's self is lost. Anyone can do it, but people who sit for a living have a distinct advantage.

 **BUDDHA BULLETS**

MEDITATION: STEP ONE

- Sit down. If you are already sitting, stay that way.

- Breathe. Breathe again. Breathing is good. Think about the alternative!

- Your goal is to reach the point where, no matter what happens in any given day, you just don't give a shit.

> *Jimmy crack corn . . . And I don't care.*
> S. FOSTER

◇ This is more difficult than one might think. It is in the nature of human beings to care about what happens to them. But this caring is a delusion and a relic of your pre-Zen existence.

◇ Remember—nothing matters. You could be the most powerful force in the universe and it still won't make a difference in the end. Because there is no difference, and there is no end. So breathe and abolish all thought from your mind. Mmmmm. Good.

◇ Abandon the yearnings that surface during your meditations, the vagrant hopes and anxieties that are based on the desire to better yourself. Give it up. Give it all up. You are not an elephant, and in that fact lies the ultimate freedom. Let the elephants worry. Not you. Be happy.

◇ And keep in mind, my friends, that everything in the universe dies. The good news is that many will do so before you do. Most of what makes you unhappy and disturbs you will therefore be dead before you are, since much of it is older and more decrepit than you. Not that you want it that way, because you want nothing. But still. They will be gone, and you'll be left to enjoy a nice Cobb salad with extra bacon.

◇ So breathe. Feel the beauty of the infinite space around your bottomless nothingness. Your self . . . your ambitions . . . your hopes and most of all your desires . . . Let them all go!

◇ And cheer up! Look on the bright side! It could be raining!

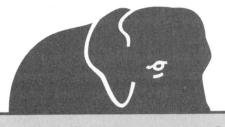

Zen and the Art of Managing Up

BASIC

HANDLING THE ELEPHANT

INTERMEDIATE

MANAGING THE ELEPHANT

ADVANCED

THROWING THE ELEPHANT

BASIC:
HANDLING THE ELEPHANT

The hands manipulate the sword, the mind manipulates the hands. Cultivate the mind and do not be deceived by tricks, feints, and schemes. They are the properties of the magician, not the samurai.

SAITO YAKURO

Keep It Simple, Stupid.

IBM SLOGAN

Before the Elephant Arrives: You

The beast has never gone astray, and what is the use of searching for him? The reason why the oxherd is not on intimate terms with him is because the oxherd himself has violated his own inmost nature.

THE TEN OXHERDING PICTURES
FIFTEENTH CENTURY JAPAN

Who . . . are . . . you?
THE CATERPILLAR, TO ALICE

What is the basic equipment you will use to manage the beast into nothingness?

Yourself.

But . . . what is that? One may not lose the self— your self, which has been with you, off and on, since birth—without fully understanding its role in your life to date.

Research shows that the self may be broken down into several component parts:

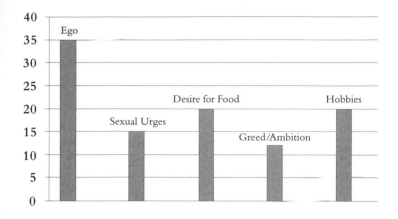

What good have any of these things done you, at least lately? Except perhaps for hobbies, each may be dispensed with at a certain age with no great loss of happiness and certainly, peace.

But . . . are you ready to do so?

Do you need your ego? Well . . . maybe. But what is it?

Ego
What is it?

- ✪ Your ego is that sense of who you are that greets you each morning when you arise from your bed. You look in the mirror and recognize what you see, unless you are a transsexual, in which case there is nothing we can do for you here.
- ✪ Your ego is what makes you proud, your sense of style, how you dress, what you feel it is appropriate to order in a restaurant, the electronics you buy to

validate yourself, the brands of the things you buy, from mozzarella cheese to flashlight batteries.

- ◇ Your ego is your sense of how much more important you are than other people, and how much less important, too.
- ◇ It is your pride over what you have achieved, and your pride over what you have not achieved and others have at a price you would not pay.
- ◇ Your ego is everything you love about yourself, and everything you love about the world around you as it cooperates in the glorious job of making you happy.
- ◇ Your ego is what you hope to achieve, the sum of all your striving and ambition.

But in truth—is not your ego also a burden? Would it not be best to leave this glut of hoping and wishing and striving and loving and hating and yearning and churning behind and simply make the journey without all that baggage? Seeing everything, marveling at everything, aware of duty and fate but free of just about everything else?

Of what use is the self?

Imagine, if you will, that there is a man, or possibly a woman, if you prefer, and he or she is driving a car down the highway. The road ahead is clear, and it is a good car, in good condition, although probably overpriced by 20 percent because it is German. Suddenly, the air bag deploys!

Several considerations now present themselves. In truth, the road ahead remains pristine and beautifully navigable. It is a good road, and safe to those who can see its twists and turns. The car remains an excellent vehicle, with perhaps a slight tendency to oversteer in the turns that is the mark of all European touring cars, but that's a matter of taste.

And yet, the driver cannot see! He is in mortal danger because this gigantic, puffy bag is in front of him. He cannot see around it! He cannot see over or under it! All he can see is the bag, which was placed there for his safety in accidents but which now serves no purpose but to obscure his view.

That bag is your self. It was needed when you were young and prone to accidents. But now it obscures the road ahead of you and makes it impossible for you to navigate the path that destiny intended for you.

Get rid of it! You can do it! And not by a step-by-step careful process, either. Now. Just drop the whole ego thing.

Once it's gone, anything is possible. The road ahead will be clear. People can insult you. Misfortune can beset you. Idiots can offend you. They can move your office. They can cut your budget. They can ignore you. They can strip you of duties. They can load you down with duties so egregiously that you scarcely ever see the sun. It won't matter. Because everything is of equal value, or no value, of equal size, and no size. There is only the enormous nothingness that lies within and without everything. And the road ahead.

BUDDHA BULLET

◑ All other aspects of your self will melt away. Only golf—the ultimate distraction—poses any danger to the Zen warrior. The rest is up to you.

Before the Elephant Arrives: It

It was like being a fly on the wall at a meeting.

*JACK WELCH ON HIS JOB AT AGE TWELVE AS A CADDY FOR
LOCAL BUSINESSMEN AT A SALEM, MASSACHUSETTS,
COUNTRY CLUB*

This is awful.

*GENERAL MILLS CEO STEPHEN W. SANGER RECALLING HIS
FIRST LAW COURSE AND THE DECISION TO SWITCH TO A
CAREER IN BUSINESS*

Elephants may be born, but they are also made, mostly by their mothers. And they leave tiny tracks on the path they have taken to get to you.

H. Ross Perot is indeed a small and stringy little elephant. He is also capable of moving larger beasts around at will, having given birth, in a miracle stunning to the political world, to the much larger and noiser Jesse Ventura. The young Perot, it is said, was given a Norman Rockwell print of a Boy Scout at prayer by his mother, who ripped the picture out of a magazine and tacked it up over the young elephant's desk. The picture became "everything I strived to be," Mr. Perot has said.

Any young monk attempting to manage Mr. Perot would do well to know that this tiny elephant has viewed himself, throughout his life, as a Boy Scout at prayer. Such information would be of tremendous leverage later. And leverage is at the heart of what we are learning.

Everyone comes from someplace. Charles F. Knight, the dynamic CEO who used to run Emerson, arguably one of the best-run companies in the world, was just fifteen when his father drove away from him, leaving him in the great and somewhat empty nation of Canada with just $100 in the bank and a summer job in a metal foundry. "Well, I'll see ya" are the words Mr. Knight remembers as the last his father ever said to him.

That's got to hurt. And yet, how big an elephant did that experience produce!

The inexperienced handler would do well, therefore, to know as much as is possible about his elephant before it enters the room. For underneath the great beast beats the heart of the child. Find that heart and you will find the first key you seek.

BUDDHA BULLET

○ There is a great worldwide web that winds its way about us. Surf that web, and you may find answers about the great gray one who is about to enter your life. Sit. Boot up. Log on. Say "Google." Hit Enter.

I was a no–date nerd.

SUN MICROSYSTEM'S BILL JOY ON BEING VOTED HIS NORTH FARMINGTON, MICHIGAN, HIGH SCHOOL'S "MOST STUDIOUS STUDENT" WHEN HE GRADUATED AT AGE FIFTEEN

When you have one eye and you're the smallest kid in the class, you've got to figure out how to get along with people, as opposed to bludgeoning your way in.

BOB PITTMAN

The calf is father to the elephant. Elephants may dispute this, wanting to believe they have somehow made themselves. But while they may have improved themselves, their elephant status was given to them by whatever forces run their cosmos, and yours.

They may believe that they have had experiences and epiphanies that shaped their lives, helped them to improve their topspin or handicap. But at bottom, no. They are born into the world small and weak, as elephants, nothing less. If you were going to be one, you would know it already. You would have known it long ago.

As you think about the elephant you are about to encounter, cast your mind back many years. Goodness, what a sad little beastie it is likely to be. For often, it is true, we find that the young elephant was a miserable creature who was deficient in some fundamental way. He or she was the shortest, the fattest, the least likely to succeed. Perhaps most wonderful is that the individual who was once considered the one most likely to succeed is now selling Toyotas on Route 22. He's good at it too, just as he was good at everything back then.

But he is not an elephant.

The wretch in the glasses with the thick lenses, the geek like Bill Joy who weighed either 90 or 290 pounds in eighth grade, it is he who now thunders down the mountain with his tusks in the air, taking on competing operating systems and daring to strike off in new directions with state-of-the-art technology.

If you doubt this, examine a picture of William Gates before he discovered that somebody had invented DOS and realized that he could buy it from them for a fraction of its value. Look at that expression, that skin, that shock of hair standing as vertical as the redwood forest. Could that be a baby elephant in the making?

Of course it could. Indeed, it was.

And you were not. You developed and changed and moderated yourself and became a competent individual in touch with your surroundings. The elephant, on the other hand, was incapable from the outset of shaping itself. It was itself, and that was that. It was for others to shape themselves to it.

Roger Ackerman, the turnaround tycoon at Corning, says he learned about stress when he made ends meet by collecting tolls at night on the Garden State Parkway near Newark, New Jersey. He took tolls, and he smiled, and he dreamed of the open plains.

Tony La Russa, manager of the St. Louis Cardinals and perhaps the greatest intellectual in the business of baseball, was a diaper folder for the company that sponsored his Pony League baseball team.

It is said that the Buddha for a time sold IBM typewriter ribbons over the telephone. This was in the dawning of the age of computers. No one had typewriters. No one needed ribbons. It was, in its essence, an activity so profoundly meaningless that it gave the Buddha a peek at the bottomless nothingness that underlies all existence. This helped him later on.

For in the end, it is all typewriter ribbons.

So calm down. Feel the lightness flow within you. And chill out, for goodness' sake.

BUDDHA BULLET

◌ Labor for its own sake is noxious. The elephant has gotten to the point where it does not need to engage in it anymore, but can simply engender it in others. That you are willing and able to do actual work gives you incredible power over a creature that by no means wishes to return to doing any.

MEETING THE ELEPHANT

On a branch perches a nightingale cheerfully singing;
The sun is warm, and a soothing breeze blows,
on the bank the willows are green;
The ox is there all by himself,
nowhere has he to hide himself;
The splendid head decorated with stately horns—
what painter can reproduce him?

THE TEN OXHERDING PICTURES

If you can't say something nice, don't say anything at all.

YOUR MOTHER

If you are a true student, you know the elephant before
it sidles up to your cubicle, blowing peanut-scented
moisture into your face. You know it because you have
studied it and prepared for it, before its arrival. And that
is good.

On the other hand, perhaps you are one of those
unfortunates whose elephant was sprung upon you by
surprise, in a merger or an internal coup d'état . . . or
maybe you are so shallow and foolish a creature that you
did not learn about the elephant when you had time to
do so and must observe your elephant as you meet it for
the first time.

Either way, there is little reason, if you are wise and

not a pinhead, to make sudden movements or emit loud noises. Elephants, as a rule, like neither. In the meeting, as in so many other beginnings and endings, stillness is all.

Look. Smell. Be alive to the possibilities. But say nothing. Do nothing. In such nothingness lies all the potentiality you desire. There will be time for action. Now is not that time.

True, you are relinquishing the opportunity to make a large and positive impression. But so what? Time has no beginning and no ending for one in a position to feel its ebb and flow. And how many are the negative impressions that may be formed by the judgmental elephant upon this first meeting?

None of these are very good. Each is quite possible, even likely. For the elephant is not prone to the formation of positive impressions. If it is forced to notice you, chances are you will piss it off.

You are not real to the elephant, so your silence does not matter. And there is no penalty for reticence. A young monk reports that he met Martha Stewart no fewer than four times before she showed a glimmer of recognition at their fifth encounter. This is not uncommon. One time, at a corporate gathering in Los Angeles, the Buddha had just such an encounter with a senior officer whose pen-and-ink portrait regularly graces the front page of the *Wall Street Journal*. "Have you ever noticed how this man, whose good opinion is so important to so many, refers to everyone he meets as 'man' or 'pal' or 'babe' and sometimes even 'dude'?" said the Buddha, smiling and shaking his head with affectionate resignation. "That is because he has no idea who he is speaking with. We are all one to him. And that makes him more powerful than anybody in this restaurant."

Potential Elephant
First Impressions of You

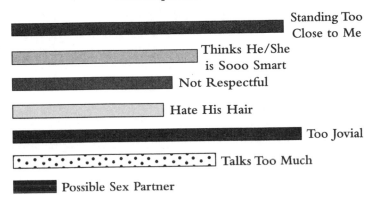

Standing Too Close to Me

Thinks He/She is Sooo Smart

Not Respectful

Hate His Hair

Too Jovial

Talks Too Much

Possible Sex Partner

You are part of the air that surrounds the elephant. Calm air is better than a storm, is it not? Do not therefore be the one to break the wind. There will come a time for that . . . in just a moment, perhaps.

BUDDHA BULLETS

◌ Attempt to look intelligent. This is not always easy, even if you are. One may appear intelligent for these purposes by thinking of something urbane, fascinating, or piquant, even slightly wicked, then pretending that it is about to cross your lips if you were not preventing it from doing so for reasons best known to yourself. For example, think this: "A rational approach to the free market mingles a certain commitment to laissez-faire capitalism with an underlying

belief in actions that serve the common good."
Alternatively, you may also think of a big plate of
fresh sushi that has one item on it you can't quite
recognize but must eat due to a business obligation to
your Japanese host. Concentrate on that item. As
long as you do not speak, you will appear intelligent
while either of these constructs is in your mind.
Later, the elephant will think back upon your meeting and wonder, "Who was that smart person who
said not a word?" or it will think nothing, and that is
all right, too.

○ Look the elephant in the eye. This is an important
part of effective quiescence. If you are silent and do
not establish eye contact, you have blown the meeting. It is possible you are not even ready to read this
book. Give it to a friend who deserves it and go sit
under a tree in the park until the seat of your pants is
wet.

○ If you are spoken to, go to the next chapter. In fact,
go there anyway. Now.

GREETING THE ELEPHANT

I noticed first of all how tiny he was, and how amazingly fresh and small his shoes were, like shoes on a mannequin in a department store. And how he walked on his toes into the meeting, like he was afraid of breaking something in his feet. Then he took my hand, and his grip was very firm, almost inhumanly firm. And he looked into my eyes, and sort of saw how weird I was finding him. And after that, we never really got along very well. I don't need to work for anybody that perceptive.

FORMER VICE PRESIDENT,
WESTINGHOUSE ELECTRIC CORPORATION,
ON MEETING THE THEN-CEO OF THE COMPANY

Elephants see a great deal. It is hard to fool them, but it is important to try. In greeting the elephant, it is once again advisable to find a place of great internal stillness from which to pop momentarily with a formal, highly structured, appropriate response.

Greetings are formal and structured occasions, where the following great cosmic principle applies:

Greeting
Effectiveness

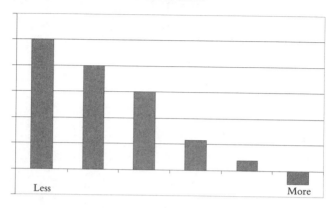

Less   More

What, however, is appropriate as a greeting? It is a question as old as time, one that has plagued the sages since Buddha sat under the bodhi tree.

The greeting offered the elephant, to be appropriate, must be correct within the context of your industry, your organization, your office work environment, and most importantly, the social context in which you are meeting on that given day.

A quick handshake and formal greeting in an elevator is appropriate. A gushing invocation of lifelong admiration for the elephant is not. That same gooey tower of flattery, on the other hand, would be fine if the elephant is encountered at an industry dinner in his honor at the Waldorf.

Understanding of the elephant's organization is almost equally crucial. When greeting an executive from General Electric, for example, it is not inappropriate to

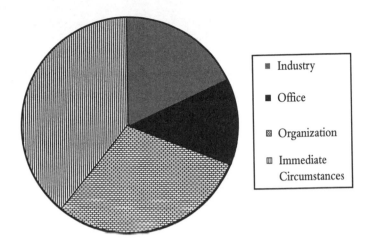

- ▪ Industry
- ■ Office
- ▨ Organization
- ▥ Immediate Circumstances

murmur something vague, indulge in one small shake of the hand, then step back with eyes averted from the brilliance of the elephant on display. This shows respect for both the elephant and the organization for which it works, the knowledge that this elephant may well be a wolf in a gray leather skin.

One would be similarly advised to adopt a moderate tone with the recent incarnation of AOLephants. Long known for their Internet informality (and the signature open-collared shirt), the current crop of conquering management is now attaining virtually Microsoftian swagger, self-importance, assertiveness, and omniscience on a wide variety of new and interesting subjects. There is only one topic that will satisfy such elephants, and that is the wisdom and superbness of their merger. "Love your merger," you may say without fear. They will take you at your word and possibly even ask you why, in which case you have begun well.

Contrarily, in greeting a football player or show-business elephant, one may be much more effusive and would not go amiss by placing a large dollop of lather over its face and scraping it off with your tongue. Famous elephants get used to that treatment and view anything less as meanness of spirit, if not lack of taste.

BUDDHA BULLETS

○ Greetings are formal and must serve a purpose. Your purpose is neither to make friends with nor to impress the elephant. The purpose is to accomplish the greeting, nothing more.

○ Focus. Stillness. Function. Let each goal take care of itself and the journey will soon be accomplished. That is as true in greeting elephants as it is in chopping an onion or making a hat-trick in hockey.

BUDDHA BONUS:
FIVE ALL-PURPOSE APPROACHES

1 Minimal: "Hello."
2 Less minimal: "Hello, sir." (But never "madam.")
3 Deferential: "Hello, Mr. Roover." (Or Ms. Roover, or more often these days, Carly or Martha or Jack or Mel or Mike or Steve or whatever nickname the elephant has adopted to make itself look like a regular guy.)

4 Obsequious: "It is a pleasure to meet you, sir. I've been a huge fan for a long time, not only of your management style, but also of your game. How do you manage to maintain a four handicap with all that you have to do?"

5 Culturally appropriate: "Yo, whazzup, ma man!"

Memorize the pitch until it flows from your mouth like carbon monoxide from the exhaust pipe of a Mack Truck.

CONFIDENTIAL AMERICAN CONTINENTAL CORPORATION MEMO TO SALESMEN OF BONDS THAT FINANCED CHARLES H. KEATING'S ILL-FATED PHOENICIAN HOTEL

Fellow Cast Members . . .

SALUTATION FROM DISNEY CHAIRMAN MICHAEL EISNER ON A MEMO TO ALL EMPLOYEES ANNOUNCING THE LAYING OFF OF FOUR THOUSAND OF THEM

While the elephant may appear to be social, it is not a joiner. It may be seen in a crowd, but for it to be happy it must be a crowd of its own devising. Others join the elephant. It does not join others.

This commitment to solitude is born of the elephant's consciousness of its size relative to others. It is simply bigger, that is all. And it knows it.

Being alone so much, the elephant develops a language, both verbal and stylistic, that you must learn if you wish to establish any sort of control over it.

Portions of this tongue are inherited from the elephants who have come before and have long since gone to the boneyard. When Disney CEO Michael Eisner informed his company by memo of the imminent layoff of some four thousand previously essential souls, he addressed them all as "Fellow Cast Members." Some might find this terminology odd, given that the communication expelled a large number of the recipients from the status in the salutation. But it was not odd. It was simply a use first coined by Walt, the original Disney, whose use of the term *cast member* went back to the early days of the studio and included anybody who was working for "the show." Later, when organizational theorists created the small, totalitarian duchy known as Disneyland, the tradition continued. Today, if you go to one of the Disney theme parks and purchase a hot dog from a stand or see your gum wrapper being swept up by a boy in a vest and top hat, those individuals are "cast members" just as surely as is the poor, sweating individual losing his sanity inside the Goofy suit on that hot August day. Anyone attempting to understand and control elephants within that company had best understand such language before attempting to get astride an elephant there or even to lead it by its nose ring.

"Learn the pitch," saith the sage. The pitch is the spoken word, offered in a structured form. Learn it. Rely on it. The pitch is a language with few words, because elephants actually have but perhaps five or six general topics in which they are interested at any point in time.

THE SIX-TIERED WEDDING CAKE OF UNIVERSAL ELEPHANT TOPICS (IN NO PARTICULAR ORDER)

GOLF: We will deal later with the role golf can play in the cosmic universe of certain elephantine imaginations. Elephants addicted to golf are like drug addicts, but the drug is not debilitating or serious in its psychological implications. It is simply a stupid aphrodisiac, like Percodan or glue. All golf addicts think about is golf. Yes, it is sad. But if you can talk golf, you can talk to this elephant.

FOOTBALL: Football, unlike golf, is not a lifestyle. It is a metaphor, a veil through which all football elephants see the world. Problems in the business? You're fourth and long. Financing fail to come through? You've been sacked! Ready to pop the big deal and achieve a substantial payday? You're in the red zone, baby, ready to punch on through to the other side!

SHAREHOLDER VALUE/STOCK PRICE: The altruistic side of greed. You are producing value for everybody but yourself, and then, when all others are accommodated, yourself, too. The language that must be learned is primarily economic in nature, but there aren't that many terms necessary for the young monk to conjure: EBITDA, cash flow, EPS, IBT, etc. It's all bushwah. The real scorecard is on the ticker every day, and in certain organizations, that's all that people talk about. The better you can talk about it, the better off you will be.

WAR: Warlike elephants see everything in terms of wins and losses, life-and-death struggles, towering enmities, loyalty, betrayal, and retribution. The language of such elephants is always supercharged with emotion. You must love that elephant, cleave to its friends with hoops of steel, and with equal verve despise its enemies. Death to the traitor! Eternal life to those who serve and die!

APPLE PIE, QUALITY, AND THE CUSTOMER:
This is perhaps the most intolerable language of all, but
in suffering there is enlightenment, so concentrate on
the little bolus of light on the inside of your forehead
and achieve quietus. Here, Brahma, as always, is in the
details. Surveys, focus groups, and other pseudoscientific
measurements prevail on this all-but-forgotten planet,
which was well populated in the 1980s, but has since
been abandoned by the greater portion of the fleet.
Here, you must study charts, attend virtual-socialist
reeducation programs dedicated to customer satisfaction,
and otherwise measure out your dedication to the elephant in coffee spoons. Learn to speak glowingly of the
customer, his or her satisfaction, and joys pertaining
thereof. That is what makes this elephant dance.

OTHER: Hunting, shooting, white-water rafting,
stamps, coins, antique cars, the situation with Dallas that
must by all means be resolved if the Blitsky deal is to be
consummated, wine, cigars, priapic sex with little people
from the circus . . . whatever is on the top of the elephant's mind that morning is what you must speak of.
Listen. When you can simulate an echo to its speech and
even add to that echo, congratulations. You are ready to
reply. Not before.

BUDDHA BULLETS

◇ Language is self. Since the elephant is all about itself, so
must be the language it speaks. Joining with the eternal, repetitive, circular mandala of its self-referential

obsessions, you step closer to your goal of elephant mastery.

○ Hear now with your Buddha ear. The elephant is speaking . . . about whales, and how they are endangered on this planet . . . about interest rates or the stock price or the cost of a meal in midtown or the breasts on that flight attendant last week. But move beyond, and above. Cast your mind into the ethosphere a thousand feet in the air above the elephant. What do you hear? Nonsense. Trumpeting. The elephant expressing itself. That's what it's all about. The elephant's self. That is the one thing to which you must speak. All else is as insubstantial as wind in the trees at night.

○ A riddle: What is of supreme importance to every person, but completely insubstantial and of no importance whatsoever unless one is an elephant?

○ The Buddha would not tell you the answer, but since this is a business book, you may know without too much contemplation. The answer is simple. It is staring back at you in the mirror. The thing that takes up no room, that is of no worth, the ultimate, transcendent empty space . . . is you. Your self. For your self, unlike the elephant self, is of no interest. It is of no importance. It is nothing. Think of that as you study the elephant's language in your first great assault to speak to it.

> You are an empty vessel. You are a medium through which things pass. You are nothing.
> What a relief!

I did not have sexual relations with that woman.

BILL CLINTON

What a terrible thing it is to lose one's mind . . . or not to have a mind at all. . . .

DAN QUAYLE

This antitrust thing will blow over.

BILL GATES TO INTEL EMPLOYEES IN 1995

And it came to pass that the Buddha was sojourning through an airport one day in the winter of a year not long past. And he was recognized by one of his disciples whose plane had been canceled by US Airways for some reason having to do with equipment, which for some reason US Airways seems to do more than others, perhaps at the bidding of a higher power seeking to remind each traveler of the arbitrariness of existence. Who knows?

And this disciple, who was rebooked on American Airlines, approached the Buddha, who was at that moment doing his best to not-think in a comfortable chair in the Admiral's Club, a complimentary orange juice and dish of mixed nuts by his side.

There may be those who wonder at the presence of

the Divine One in surroundings of such ostensible opulence. Of course, it is not for you to wonder, but there are reasons that may be instructive to you, so you shall know.

First of all, a lot of very ordinary and even shabby people find their way into the first-class club at any airport for reasons that are unclear, so the area in truth was much like any other, only quieter, and that is good for anyone, even the Buddha. Second, the Buddha had at that time entered the higher state of consciousness in which he had come to view unnecessary self-abnegation as a form of personal indulgence, and reasonable comfort as an aid to complete understanding of the cosmos, as it is written in his fabled sutra on the importance of suitable office furniture: "He whose lower back is messed up from cheap or inadequate seating cannot leave his body for more important work." Thus was the Buddha in the Admiral's Club, working to achieve his customary state of grace. And now you know.

"Lord," said the acolyte. "Why would the airline cancel a flight with more than one hundred people whose lives depend on getting where they are supposed to be? This is not the first time US Airways has done this, either! One suspects they cancel flights if they are not sufficiently booked to achieve a profitable margin!"

The Buddha smiled and offered the mendicant a nut. "Take a nut," he said. The business monk did as he was instructed, and then the Buddha added, as if as an afterthought, "Elephants do not think about the consequences of their actions," he said. "They dwell primarily on the goals they believe they must achieve because of their greatness, weight, and infallibility. That is why everywhere the elephant goes, even though it goes in splendor and light, it leaves behind a trail of destruction and waste that must be cleaned up by its handlers."

"But is this fair, Lord?" said the monk, who had in truth lost his composure along with the chance for a lucrative meeting in the city to which he was sojourning. "Should not the elephant live with the consequences of its actions?"

"Fair?" said Buddha, and then he laughed so hard that he nearly choked on a filbert and had to be struck smartly in the back. "Don't do that to me again," he said to the acolyte when he had regained his divine breath.

Why did William Jefferson Clinton, upon leaving office with some small shred of reputation and legacy left to him, pardon Marc Rich, a deeply unattractive, corrupt, international criminal with virtually no friends in the media? Was it good for Clinton? Did he think about what he was doing? Did he think at all?

Why did Jerry Levin engineer the liquidation of Time Warner to AOL for no premium to its shareholders and to the great discomfort of a large body of his highly professional employees? In just a few weeks after the deed, the Internet crashed and the conquering on-line company might well have been at his feet. Was it wise? Was he thinking? Or was he simply an elephant, dreaming . . .

Why did William Gates, who seems to evince the qualities of a very intelligent person some of the time, endanger his company by predatory and anticompetitive zeal? Why did foolish numskulls at Firestone approve substandard tires for use in the United States, where such things are noticed? Why did a host of sober, eminently reactionary investment bankers and analysts approve Internet business plans and initial public offerings that were clearly born of greed and madness? Why did Richard Nixon approve a tape machine in the Oval Office, where he was accustomed to curse like a victim of Tourette's syndrome and plot the illegal destruction of his adversaries? Why did Rudolph Giuliani, the mayor of the City of New York, publicly announce his impending divorce before he had informed his media-savvy wife of his intention to do so? Why, in the not-too-distant past, did so many corporations dump lethal chemicals in the neighborhoods around their plants in full knowledge that such hazardous waste would one day poison the very ground upon which their companies were built?

The answer to all these questions is this: they are elephants, one and all. Elephants are large, with big, flat feet, and they tread much underfoot as they go along. Because they eat a tremendous amount, they also tend to leave an unconscionable amount of waste in their wake.

And who is there to clean up that waste? The elephant? Ha! No such thing. Wrap your no-mind around it. Most of your activity, particularly in the beginning of your time in service, will take place behind the elephant. They do their thing or, at times, things. We clean up after them. That is the law of nature, or at least of elephants.

On the bright side, or at least the other side, the most fertile ground lies where the elephant has been. It is your place, at least for now. Go there, and go with dharma.

BUDDHA BULLETS

◯ Make sure to dress right. It's messy back there.

◯ Do not attempt to shift this burden to others until there are others who would gladly do the work in your place. Delegation is one thing. Getting others to accomplish the Duty that should be yours is no-Zen.

◇ If you are filled with shame or resentment at the task, you are still obviously filled with the burden of self and will be unable to move farther down the path. There is no shame here, because shame comes with self, and you have no self. Be courageous, therefore, and rejoice. Stand tall, except when you must bend over for a pickup. As always, do your job.

◇ In the work, whatever work that may be, there is Buddha.

Feeding the Elephant

The one sure way to conciliate a tiger is to allow oneself
to be devoured.

Konrad Adenauer

Where the wheel turns
The void gnashes its teeth.

Daito Kokushi

The wheel turns. The void gnashes its teeth. And if you
are not careful, little flower waiting to pop its first bud,
that void will gnash all over you. Being gnashed is
unpleasant and should be avoided at all cost. The power
of dharma can assist you in the avoidance of all gnashing,
inflicted by others or generated by the remains of your
annoyingly persistent self.

Feeding that void is one of the first things you must
learn as you make your way down the path, for only
when one has mastered the feeding of the elephant may
one move on to higher levels of control.

Elephants do not feed as fast as wolves or tigers. They
are large animals and their appetites may vary depending
on their size and the time of day. But within every elephant is a gigantic void that must be fed. By you.

Before you run out to purchase the world's largest
hibachi, take a moment and attain inner focus. Sit, if by

chance you are not already sitting. Breathe and consider. Ah! Now you see, do you not?

What you are meant to feed is not the elephant's stomach, my little charbroiled shrimp. An elephant can always take care of that. What you are responsible for feeding is its ego, its imagination, its ambition, its hopes, its fears when that is to your advantage. You are meant to feed the elephant's soul.

Yes, chicklet. It is true. Elephants do have souls, and their souls are never larger than when they are being fed. So feed them! And well and often! For if you do not, it will do one of two things:

1 Accept food from other handlers, making your role questionable at best.
2 Eat you.

What, then, should the elephant be fed? What indeed! There are so many alternatives, for all elephants are omnivores. The specific diet and timing would certainly seem to depend on the elephant. But what does it want? When does it want it? This may be difficult to ascertain and be unknown even to the beast itself. The elephant that this morning was quite satisfied with a pile of soft numbers and cheese may suddenly appear in the afternoon trumpeting for hard research material and quantifiable action. You don't want that.

You want the elephant to be consistent, tractable, and in the end, wise. Its diet can be a major assistance in that regard, and a force for chaos and change if you do not do things right.

Here are some dietary guidelines that apply to all but the most unusual elephants.

Mornings: Offer a variety of choice information with their hay, provided in the form of news clippings, faxes, memos, telephone communications, and even the traditional hand feeding of data nuggets at daybreak. Not everything you give must be sweet and juicy. If what is on hand is bitter and tough to swallow, such is the fare that must be offered that day. Silence is the only substance on which an elephant cannot be nourished, for silence does nothing to fill that void and put off potential gnashing.

Late morning: Give the elephant a small snack of good news about itself or bad news about others. This will often hold it until lunch.

Midday often finds your elephant grazing where it pleases, and it may require no additional assistance from you, as it munches its turkey hash or plows through a Cobb salad the size of Kansas in the company of other elephants large and small.

If, on the other hand, it is not a popular elephant or is reclusive in some way, it may be fed a friendly fax or E-mail or a careful visit to the lonely elephant who is sitting at its desk, slurping up a solitary carton of wonton soup. At this time, or in the early afternoon when the elephant is trying to find a reason not to nap, a well-timed joke can do wonders.

At some time during the day, whether it is in the very early morning or the late afternoon, the elephant will demand a full ration of meat. This will take the form of an issue, opportunity, or danger upon which the elephant must act. Take care when approaching the elephant at this juncture. It is the most important feeding of the day, and it is likely to take off your arm if you don't accomplish the task in a precise and correct fashion. We may refer to this as the Business Feeding, and is different from all others, as it is written in the *Dhammapada*:

> Let one be watchful of speech irritation. Let him practice restraint of speech. Having abandoned the sins of speech, let him practice virtue with his speech.

That is, you must not feed your bulky friend the wrong way, and at the same time you must also take care to feed it the right way. Simply being careful and Not Wrong is not enough. You must, as the path before you, be Right.

At the end of day—or if your elephant is nocturnal, then in early morning—there is also a time when it is appropriate to allow others to handle the feeding. The truth is, elephants eat all day long. Your task is to make sure that its favorite and most essential meals are the ones you, and no one else, are providing.

BUDDHA BULLET

TENTATIVE FEEDING SCHEDULE

Time	Nature	Purpose
1st Feeding, 6:30 A.M.	Short update (voice mail)	Shows you are up early and thinking about elephant needs
2nd Feeding, 8:20 A.M.	Drop by with data nugget	Shows you are in early
3rd Feeding, 10:13 A.M.	Faxed cartoon from *The New Yorker*	Shows you share zeitgeist with elephant

Time	Nature	Purpose
4th Feeding, 1:13 P.M.	Drop by with sheaf of research material (elephant not in)	Shows you are working through lunchtime on important stuff
5th Feeding 2:40 PM	Return with research material, have brief discussion	Shows you risk being pesky due to importance of your agenda
6th Feeding 4:00 PM	Force-feed elephant, (by cc, with attachment) a thick paste of tasteless, gooey mung	Shows elephant you are extraordinarily serious.
7th Feeding 5:30 PM (Mandatory)	Present elephant with bad problem that must be addressed, and to which you have a solution	Shows elephant you are handling critical material and that you are indispensable at solving problems that he only knows about when you bring them to his attention.
8th Feeding 7:00 PM (Optional)	Good-night sweetmeat	Shows elephant you care

○ As ever, tiny dragon, you exist to be a student of this elephant, and of all others. Know its likes and dislikes. A few nuts in your pocket may do more for you in the long run than a backpack full of stew.

WATERING THE ELEPHANT

> I realized that there are gloves that do things that other
> gloves can't possibly do, like let you stick your hand in
> hydrochloric acid.
>
> *MARTHA STEWART*

Elephants have odd needs. Beyond their hunger to fill the void, they have a thirst for the exceptional that you, young and all-but-eyeless spud, must help them quench.

Why would Martha Stewart want to stick her hand in hydrochloric acid? Doesn't she have enough to do? Of course she does. She has a magazine to run. A television show to produce. She is everywhere at once, from stuffing shallots into a pig to making a wreath from barbed wire. . . .

But if you work for Martha Stewart, you must be aware that, at times, she may wish to immerse her hand in skin-devouring, bone-dissolving hydrochloric acid.

You cannot venture to tell Martha Stewart that it might be best to forgo altogether the plunging of her hand into hydrochloric acid, even if there are gloves that would make it possible for her to do so.

It is equally pointless for you to reason with Martha Stewart, to try to help her see that many people live their entire lives without sticking their hands into hydrochloric acid, and that she, above many, need not be one who does so, given all that she has going on.

It is not even expected that you volunteer to do the thing yourself, for Martha Stewart desires not that you should stick your hand in the hydrochloric acid. This elephant wants to do it herself.

Your job is simple: help her find the gloves and, possibly, procure the hydrochloric acid.

When the elephant finds the gloves and knows the acid is at hand if the urge arises, the elephant will then know it is ready for the impossible. And your job, invisible and insignificant one, will be accomplished.

BUDDHA BULLETS

- ◌ Question not the elephant's thirst. There are many yearnings known only to those with tusks. Elephants do not live by food alone.

- ◌ Quench the thirst and you will be loved by the elephant more than if you fed it for years on the choicest of table scraps.

POLISHING THE ELEPHANT'S TUSKS

> For some reason many people think of me as lucky.
> When I walk down the street, people come up and start
> touching me.
>
> DONALD TRUMP

> All of a sudden, I notice that he is lagging behind, and he
> has his arm draped around my plant manager. He was
> kind of seducing him to put more flavorings on his brand.
> He was just more aggressive and more pushy than any-
> body else.
>
> PRODUCTION CHIEF FOR FRITO-LAY ABOUT HIS BOSS, ROGER
> ENRICO, THE FUTURE HEAD OF PEPSI, WHEN THE LATTER WAS
> AT THE COMPANY'S SNACK DIVISION IN THE MIDSEVENTIES.

Elephants! How dirty they get! It is in their very elephant nature to do so. Dirty with the mud of its travels. Dirty with the dirt of its own intense and incessant creation. Dirty because it has its arm around so many shoulders in the getting and giving of advice and orders, its hand in so many others, before the day is done. The elephant is in the face of creation all day long! How is it to remain crisp and clean without your attention?

As a beginning handler, keeping your elephant free from dirt and grime, both psychic and real, is the next step along your path toward the light.

This is not easy. Elephants touch all, and all touches the elephant. Even a big gray beast like Donald Trump, who has in the past complained about the personal hygiene implications of the common handshake and avoids them as much as he can, is touched by the impurities of the world.

As Kao-feng has said: "The whole world is a fire pit; attaining what state of mind can you avoid being burned?"

It's a trick question even for those with greater Zen chops than you. In only one state of mind does fire burn without leaving ash and can elephants be touched without being soiled. That is the Zen state of mind. As it is written: "Only the Zen bathtub has no unsightly ring."

How does one get close enough to an elephant to polish its tusks or give it a good hosing down? This would seem to be a simple process, described as follows:

- Approach the elephant
- Notice the dirt
- Offer to remove the dirt
- Remove the dirt

And yet, it is by no means as clean and clear as that. The cleaning of an elephant is an intimate act, even if all you are doing is taking a push broom to its haunches.

This concept may perhaps be expressed best in graphical terms.

Cleaning Opportunities

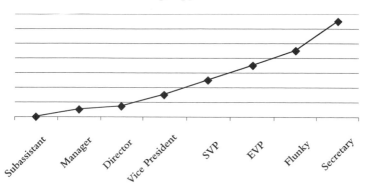

The opportunities for you, then, little sparrow, are few and far between, while those that accrue to a personal assistant or full-time flunky are many and varied, so great, in fact, that they are probably resented. You, on the other hand, must make the most of yours. Follow your Zen mind in the following progression:

WAIT WHILE NOT WAITING: It is ignoble to wait for the opportunity to clean the elephant. Therefore you will not wait, and the opportunity will come along, particularly if you are a consultant. When the time does come:

REMOVE THE ERRANT HAIR: When the elephant looks around, prepared to gore you, simply say, "Hair." And move a step backward. If this is accepted, you will then be free to move to the next step:

FLICK DANDRUFF: If you see some. This is often the first foray for the young cleanser and cannot be resented by any but the most insane elephant, particularly if it is wearing a dark suit. It is a rather presumptuous action, however, and must be well timed—that is, by being untimed. Do not plan! Planning is Not Zen! Simply act without thinking when the dandruff presents itself. Beyond that lies:

THE SPOT ON THE TIE: You may offer your own, but only in a spontaneous act. You should probably be sure that your tie is suitable for the elephant. As it is written, a young monk was attending on a great elephant, along with a friend and rival in the organization. The elephant soiled its tie immediately before it was to enter an important meeting. The first monk, who was pure in spirit and moved by the opportunity presented to him, removed his tie and grandly offered it to the elephant. "That is the ugliest tie I have ever seen," said the elephant. "Will you take mine, sir?" said the other monk, who was equally pure in spirit and cannot be criticized in any way for his equally right action. "Okay," said the elephant, putting on the second tie. Later that year, the second monk was promoted and the first monk was not.

THE ERRAND: Fetching dental floss . . . going to pick up the hairstylist, if one is in Los Angeles . . . no job is too small because small and large do not exist, are all one. The bug who brings the elephant a lump of sugar is often more highly regarded than the one mini-mammoth who presents it with a sixty-page PowerPoint presentation with depressing numbers in it.

FULL BODY WASH: Sometimes necessary for those in the highest levels of corporate life and, of course, politics. You are not ready for such work yet. Be not impatient!

◆ Confine yourself to a light tusk polishing and save the heavy lifting for those more senior than you in the great Chain of Life™.

◆ Focus your objectives. Do not clean what you cannot reach or you might fall into the bucket.

COMPLIMENTING THE ELEPHANT: LEVEL ONE

Commend a fool for his wit, or a knave for his honesty,
and they will receive you into their bosoms.

HENRY FIELDING

Donald Trump likes to refer to himself as "The Trump-
ster" . . . his organization's headquarters are lined with
framed magazine covers, each a shot of Trump or someone who looked an awful lot like him.

THE NEW GILDED AGE
AS REVIEWED IN USA TODAY

One summer evening around dusk, when the birds were
singing their last song in the tree and the heat was rising
up off the planet like a blanket no longer desired, the
Buddha was approached near the watercooler by a young
vice president. "Divine One!" said the vice president by
way of greeting. "You look excellent! Excellence is your
middle name! How wonderful and marvelous it is to be
in your presence! Can I get you anything?"

"Okay," said the Buddha. "Bring me a diet Pepsi."

After the fawning one scuttled away to procure the
beverage, one of the Buddha's senior staff approached
and, with a disgusted expression, queried the Master
about his seeming acceptance of the young wormling.

"I want a Pepsi," said the Buddha. "Why should he
not get it just as well as you? He is certainly as qualified

for the position." Then the Buddha laughed heartily and said, "Now get me the first-quarter numbers."

The elephant will be honored by those who quiver beneath it. That is its due. There are elephants who claim that they value opinions contrary to their own and tolerate those who contradict them. But these elephants are lying, whether they know it or not. Some truths for the beginner:

- Elephants have a lot of ideas. They like their own ideas, at least at first, and do not appreciate having them evaluated objectively by their handlers.
- Because they are so large, they need large amounts of praise.
- Inside every elephant, no matter how grand and confident, is a saggy, baggy, little elephant in need of validation.
- Elephants are tough on the outside and tender on the inside, like a well-cooked sirloin.
- Many elephants, on their way to the attainment of their divine status, had to butter up the larger elephants that shaped their destiny. Now that they are in a position to demand it, they expect the same treatment from the little people who serve them.

In recent years, Carly Fiorina became the head of Hewlett-Packard. But she was not always such. There was a time, not long ago, when she was looking up at the elephant from a post at Lucent, which has been proven to be no place to be at all.

When the possibility of attaining elephant status at HP first arose, Ms. Fiorina identified a key member of the Hewlett-Packard board, Dick Hackborn, a former executive vice president and author of the company's successful desktop printer business. In her second meeting with Hackborn, the aspiring elephant said that if she became CEO, she wanted him to be chairman. "This came as a complete surprise," says Hackborn, moved by the compliment. Who among us is not? When the time came when his support was needed, it was there.

Do not resist your impulse to compliment the elephant. You are right. It does expect it. And appreciate it. And it will believe anything reasonable (and even unreasonable) you say. Yes, some deplore the practice of complimenting elephants in some misguided stab at integrity. This is just an expression of self and should be rejected. Have it your way:

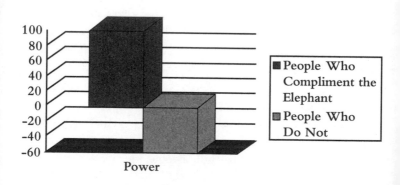

BUDDHA BULLET

◆ As in all things, accomplish the action without seeming to accomplish it. If the elephant can see what you are doing in its rearview mirror, you are too close.

REJOICING WITH THE ELEPHANT WHEN IT IS HAPPY

Last year at a Seattle restaurant to celebrate Amazon's big junk-bond offering (the first by an Internet company), CFO Joy Covey joined her boss on the floor for a round of leg wrestling. She won.

FORTUNE

Joy Covey knew her elephant well—well enough to know the happy little Bezos would not mind losing a leg-wrestling contest with his CFO. When the elephant wants to have fun, it is best to fully engage in the fun, not to distance oneself from it. This does not apply to scheduled fun such as golf or budget reviews of others, but rather to genuine celebration that bonds one to one's elephant in hoops of shared joy.

The event can be small or large. In his younger years, throughout his travels in search of enlightenment, the Buddha often found himself in the service of elephants who obtained huge pleasure from newspaper reports that were damaging to the reputations of their competitors and even, in Los Angeles, their friends. "Here," the Buddha would exclaim, handing a clip from *Variety* to his elephant of the moment. "You are going to love this very much."

And the elephant would love it very much. And at the same time, would love Buddha, too. And loving the Buddha can never be bad.

The happy elephant is an easy thing to handle. One chairman of a rust-belt corporation liked to drink Scotch whiskey and play the jazz piano. Those who served him simply had to drink and sing. There are more difficult tasks.

In his joy at the demise of his cochairman, Sanford Weill of Citigroup held a festive gathering at which he dressed as Moses and celebrated the defeat of Pharaoh. Those who attended were simply required to do nothing but laugh. And, of course, drink.

Drink is often involved when elephants dance.

What does your elephant like to do when the joy is upon it? Can you manage to be around when that time arrives? Being around is the first requirement of Zen service. One cannot do nothing effectively if one is not around to not do it.

There are dangers when the elephant is in its joyful, playful mood, however. When it flails about recklessly, hallooing and making jolly noises, one must stand back for fear of being trampled.

Several years ago, at a dinner in downtown Chicago, a group of senior monks well known to the Buddha gathered around two of the big elephants who ran their lives at that moment in circus history. One was departing for the great elephant graveyard back at the home office. The new elephant was coming in to take his place. There was much trumpeting and consumption of beverages, and before anyone knew it, the departing elephant, full of good spirits and reckless abandon, had turned over the dining room table at the restaurant and destroyed about $100,000 worth of antique furniture. If one of his handlers had not been the designated driver that night, there would have been no one to negotiate with the police who had been called, and the entire senior management structure of the corporation would have been arrested!

You too can be the Zen mind in such situations without being a negative presence in the universe. Keep your distance when the noise gets high. Intrude yourself if the situation looks as if it might get out of hand and injury might be done to the elephant.

But do nothing to postpone or dampen the triumphant feelings that all too rarely transform the beast and those who serve it into living expressions of the happy oneness of the cosmos.

Nobody, and certainly not the Buddha, who was as big a fan of joy as anybody you can think of, likes a party pooper.

BUDDHA BULLET

◇ In the elephant's joy is another opportunity to lose your self. Seize it!

> My motto is "Living is limitless," okay, and because it's
> limitless, my day will never end, my opportunities will
> never end.
>
> *MARTHA STEWART*

Elephants have outsize hopes, expectations, and dreams. It is only natural, then, that they will often be disappointed by the real world outside themselves. When the self is so great, it must inevitably come into contact with the hard truth that it is not the center of the universe, that days do end, eventually, as do opportunities.

One must love the elephant for its boneheaded refusal to accept its own nothingness. One must resist elephant thinking in oneself. Only in this way can one help the elephant in times of loss and disappointment.

Perhaps the most poignant thing about elephants is that, in spite of their size, power, and majesty that surpasses all understanding . . . they do cry. Elephants incarcerated in cages at the zoo shed tears. Elephants separated from their young do as well. And elephants who believe that the world will conform itself to their greatness have been seen, dejected and alone, weeping for the loss of the illusion that their self is in control of the cosmos. Alexander the Greek shed tears when he had no more worlds to conquer. Ted Turner, the ousted titan of Time Warner, the largest landholder in the United States, who patterns himself on Alexander the Great, sobbed profusely and openly at a private screening of *The Iron Giant,* a cartoon produced by his studio. Of course, Turner is a very thoughtful elephant and perhaps overly prone to melancholia and contemplation.

Unfortunately for any monk who is in the neighborhood, the other side of the sad elephant is the angry elephant. For the beginner, there is but one Zen solution to the problem of the angry elephant. To be Not There. Later, we will find other answers.

Before that moment arrives, however, one has a responsibility to serve the sad creature who is in your care. The events and situations that may make an elephant unhappy are almost impossible to measure. They are as numberless as the stars!

Let us count a few of them:

- A business deal falls through that would have made the elephant a lot of money. For a moment, it is clear that things are not ordered the way the elephant has thought. It is sad.
- A newspaper article or CNBC segment insults the elephant or aggrandizes the elephant's enemy. For a moment, it is clear that not everyone in the external world marches to the melody sung by the elephant. It is sad.
- The Cobb salad ordered by the elephant does not have a sufficient quantity of bacon bits. This makes the elephant feel less important. And it is sad.
- An employee whom the elephant has valued declares his intention to leave the herd. The ele-

phant has created the world around it to conform to its needs and perception of its greatness. Why would anyone want to leave? This makes the elephant very sad.

- The elephant has caught a glimpse of itself in the mirror at an unguarded moment and realizes that it is no longer young and thin, but is, in fact, somewhat hairless and paunchy. The aura of invincibility that the elephant has created for itself is, for a moment, punctured, and it feels, temporarily, simply human. This is intolerable to the elephant, and it feels extremely sad for a time.

- The stock is down after the elephant has spent several hours with security analysts. This has the potential to make the elephant not only sad, but angry and vengeful.

One of the best times to be with the elephant is when it is angry and vengeful . . . toward somebody else. But that is another story.

When the elephant is simply sad, there are things that one may do, all of which derive from the one righteous path:

- Keep company. One may sit with an elephant in silence while the elephant broods. Bring paperwork to make it look like business.

- Make conversation. Elephants have enthusiasms. Jerry Seinfeld collects cars in a big garage somewhere in California. He is likely to talk about them when he is feeling vulnerable. Jack Welch, of course, is a famous golfer. Golfers will talk about golf if the boat around them is taking on water and going vertical. Mr. Turner is one of the great internationalists and environmentalists in the world. He will certainly talk about global cooperation in defense of the environment if you are with him when he is sad. Others are simply content to talk about interest rates or their own personal fortunes. The notion of wealth that will outlast current difficulties often does much to dry an elephant's tears.

BUDDHA BULLETS

○ What draws on your elephant's inner child? Playing a game? Listening to music? Hearing tales of the destruction of its friends and enemies?

○ You must build its self back to the point where it once again achieves elevation.

○ In the aggrandizement of its self, the elephant finds power and happiness. Help it find that, and you will be one step closer to making the elephant fly.

On the Importance of Enthusiasm

You've got to get excited. That's how innovations happen.

Stephen Sanger
CEO, General Mills

Do you know how much faster I can fix an airplane when
I want to fix it than when I don't want to fix it?

Gordon M. Bethune
CEO, Continental Airlines

You are not a genius. You are not a giant. You are not
one of those who run and maintain the machinery of
existence. You are simply you.

There are those who shape the cosmos. There are
those who operate the gears and levers that turn reality
from one vector to another. You are not one such. You
are simply you.

You are not an elephant. You are not even a baby
elephant. You are simply one of those whose karma it is
to strain and bend, to lead by indirection, to leverage
forces infinitely more powerful than you to live their
lives to the best possible purpose. You serve. You follow. In the eye of Brahma, you are but one of those little motes that lurk around on the edge of sight, only to
disappear when regarded directly. You are simply you. A
ball of energy. A flash of light. Nothing more.

So smile. You'll live longer.

INTERMEDIATE:
MANAGING THE ELEPHANT

Life is like unto a long journey with a heavy burden. Let thy step be slow and steady, that thou stumble not. Persuade thyself that imperfection and inconvenience are the natural lot of mortals, and there will be no room for discontent, neither for despair. When ambitious desires arise in thy heart, recall the days of extremity thou have passed through. Forbearance is the root of quietness and assurance forever. Look upon the wrath of the enemy. If thou knowest not what it is to be defeated, woe unto thee, it will fare ill with thee. Find fault with thyself rather than with others.

IEYASU TOKUGAWA
SIXTEENTH CENTURY

TRUSTING THE ELEPHANT

When you say that you agree to a thing in principle, you
mean that you have not the slightest intention of carrying
it out.

OTTO VON BISMARCK

It is possible—indeed, it is necessary at times—to trust
the elephant. One may not go about the business of
managing the beast with total suspicion turning the
heart's blood to wormwood.

And yet, we have already learned that elephants
speak their own language and will, to find a peanut hidden beneath the credenza, stomp even the most beloved
and loyal handler into a lumpy mass the consistency of
library paste.

One must, therefore, do as the Buddha told his followers one afternoon over a plate of mussels at the appe-
tizer bar of the Trattoria Del Arte restaurant in New
York City. "One must," he said, cracking the shell open
and extracting the tender meat within, "trust the elephant as far as one may throw it." His followers laughed
at first, as they always did upon first hearing one of the
Buddha's observations, but afterward a conclave was
held among them and they realized the Buddha was
quite in earnest.

One must trust the elephant as far as one may throw it. How are we to understand this dictum?

If the elephant has infinite weight to you . . . then you must not trust it. For indeed it is not inherently trustworthy. The elephant thinks well of itself, believes itself to be trusting and worthy of like confidence. When asked whether she trusted the people she worked with, for example, former Warnaco chairman and CEO Linda Wachner replied, "I don't think it's so much trust as respect for other people's intellect and judgment." Now, those who have worked with the elephant in question know that she has at no time shown any respect for other people's intellect and judgment, nor any regard for them as individuals or, for that matter, slaves or vassals. The executive suite in her corporation, particularly at the level that reported to her directly, churned like a trailer in a tornado. From this we learn the truth of Buddha's observation "The elephant often believes it fits into a size-six cocktail dress. But you don't have to."

That the elephant believes itself worthy of trust is a large spiritual asset to you. It also needs to believe in the idea that it has a team poised and pleased to lead it, feed it, water it, enjoy its company, love it, live by its precepts, be guided by its needs.

In August of 2000, Sandy Weill, the Moses of Citigroup, told the *New York Times Magazine,* "The enemy is the guy down the street, not the one in the next office." This was almost immediately after he destroyed John Reed, the guy in the next office.

Is it possible, then, to trust such a beast?

Certainly. The Buddha makes this clear: it is possible to trust the elephant . . . as far as one may throw it.

This is the first time we have come face-to-face with the need actually to throw the elephant, even a short distance. But you are an Intermediate handler now. And it is time to begin taking some simple steps toward mastery.

Take a moment. Feel yourself. Feel the air around yourself. Is it not different from what it was before you began your training? Is it not a bit . . . lighter? More pure? Feel the space about you. Is it not a little bit . . . wider? Is not the sky a little taller? Brighter?

Test yourself. You have met the elephant. You have provided it with nourishment. You have rejoiced with it in its happiness. You have soothed it when it was sad.

Now, my small oyster, take a breath. Place both hands on the gray wall that is the elephant's side. And . . . push. What's that?! Did the elephant not . . . budge a tiny bit? Yes, it did. You have reached the point where the elephant will shift a small amount when you lean your full weight upon it.

Calculate the amount you can move the creature. And that is the amount you can allow yourself to indulge in trust. Or as it is written:

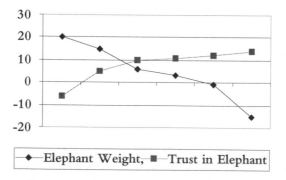

Thus it is, as it is said, the lighter the elephant to you, the more it may be trusted. Further, once a certain moderate level of trust has been reached, it is difficult to justify more. Trust plateaus, and if you are fortunate in your elephant, stays there. We may also perceive that it is possible to invest a small amount of trust in the beast even when it possesses a certain amount of weight.

What, then, may we be permitted to trust the elephant to do?

- Say what it means if it is in its best interest to do so.
- Do what it says it is going to do within a span of five to ten minutes.
- Take care of you, if you force it to do so, and not too often.
- Be true to its own nature, that is, to eat when it is hungry, drink what it likes when it likes, and lose its temper when its desires are not immediately met.
- Hate its adversaries and love those who join it in its hatreds both petty and substantial.
- Be consistent in the forms of management it will and will not tolerate.

We have spent some time on this issue of trust, because it is important. Your relationship with your elephant need not, indeed cannot be, one of mistrust, coldness, and lack of empathy. Elephants need a hospitable environment for their comfort, and you as the handler simply cannot live in an atmosphere devoid of appropriate affection and trust.

As always, take the Middle Path. On one end there is gross suspiciousness and lack of empathy. On the other, there is the supreme and total confidence one may feel for one's dog, unless that dog is under ten pounds and requires professional grooming. In trust, as in all other matters, invest what is appropriate and keep your mind's eye focused both to the left and to the right.

BUDDHA BULLET

◇ Even the lightest elephant is completely untrustworthy when it gets heavy on you.

OBEYING THE ELEPHANT

Long is the chain of existence to the foolish who do not
know the true law.

THE DHAMMAPADA

I don't care how you do it, I just want you to fuck him up.

MEDIA INDUSTRY EXECUTIVE, ANGRY THAT HIS HEAD OF
FINANCE HAD QUIT TO JOIN ANOTHER CORPORATION

The true law is that there is a law, and that the law must
be obeyed. The elephant who is thwarted is not a pretty
sight.

Not long ago, a bodhisattva out in the western region
was guilty of not attending to certain details to the complete satisfaction of his elephant. He simply didn't obey
in the right fashion, and the situation to which he should
have attended did not unfold as the elephant would have
wished. When the elephant found out, he was disappointed. He went to the office of the young monk and,
without comment, wrapped his trunk around the offending neck and choked the monk until his career was dead.

It is simple, then. The elephant must be obeyed, and
obeyed to its satisfaction.

How is one to obey the elephant to perfection?—
that is the question. There are as many ways to obey the
elephant as there are to disobey it, and in that variety lies

enlightenment, power, and control of the forces that guide the cosmos.

Only a fool or a slave obeys when ordered to do so. The seeker of truth uses the requirement as an opportunity to build power and enhance the beauty of existence.

Here, then, are Buddha's Six Pillars of Obeying™, as taught by the master immediately after a nice luncheon at Spago in Los Angeles.

BUDDHA BULLETS

THE SIX PILLARS OF OBEYING

◇ *ONE MAY OBEY SLOWLY.* To obey is inevitable. To delay is sublime. Keeping the elephant waiting is perhaps the most dangerous but most effective way to establish and prove one's importance, competence, and courage.

◇ *ONE MAY OBEY QUICKLY.* In speed too there is power, as long as the speed does not convey the impression that the task was too easy or that one's level of concern is not great enough. It is possible to communicate many things through speed—from contempt to the greatest possible regard. Never perform quickly out of fear. But as a flourish? A gesture of éclat? An expression of pure excellence? By all means, little one.

◇ *ONE MAY OBEY PARTIALLY.* A perilous game, to be sure. But sometimes the elephant issues incomplete instructions, or instructions that, if followed completely, would lead to disaster. In such cases, a partial response is a most eloquent statement.

◇ *ONE MAY OBEY BADLY.* Do you enjoy fetching the master's nose ring? The Buddha, when young, was often instructed by his wife to wash badly burned cooking pots, since they were indeed burned by his divine inattention to detail. He did clean the pots, but so badly that they had to be cleaned again by more competent hands. In this case, bad performance was an important tool to control and shape the requirements of the future.

◇ *ONE MAY OBEY WITH FULL HEART.* There are times, however, when obedience is an expression of love and may fully be appreciated as such by both elephant and handler alike. These are wonderful times and must be treasured. In great reporting relationships, as the Buddha has said, "The happy ant loves not only the queen it serves but also the lump of sugar that it carries." It is true that some measure of devotion and affection may color all of one's actions. This is an excellent thing, but not the highest form of obedience—for in love there is desire, and in the desires of this earth there is suffering. The highest form of service and obedience resides, as always, in the understanding of the emotionless, passionless, formless, painless void from which the universe was created and into which it will go, as will we, when the time comes.

◇ *ONE MAY OBEY WITH TRUE EMPTINESS.* There is the elephant. There is the task. The task must be accomplished. No anxiety shapes us. No desire drives us. The thing must be done. And by our doing it, so it is done. The spirit, moved this way and that by the exigencies of the task itself, the task *soi-même,* lapses back upon its completion into that most perfect of states, the only one from which, when the time comes, the elephant may be hoisted and thrown—the state of attention, the state of being prepared, the state, that is, of Nothingness.

If I don't obey, what can they do? I decided, there's no more following the rules.

AMAZON CFO JOY COVEY, ON DEALING
WITH HER PARENTS

If you don't have tension and you don't have confronta-tion and you don't have discussion, you're not going to grow.

MARTHA STEWART

Those who work for Martha Stewart might blink with thoughtful surprise as they learn of their master's attitude toward the value of confrontation. But as the Buddha observed in the steam room of the Boca Raton Hotel and Spa one day after an eight-hour meeting with a large group of nasty elephants, "There is confrontation and dis-cussion . . . and then there is confrontation and discussion! One must be able to ascertain the difference between the two." Those who do not know the difference will perish.

All elephants, in their hearts, have contempt for those who are overly obedient. They themselves have no such problem. From Joy Covey sassing her parents to Dubya hammering down a last brewsky before stepping into his teen hot rod to Bill Clinton taking one risk too many in the Oval Office . . . each elephant knows that to be true to his or her elephant nature means to play by nobody's rules but one's own.

So when the elephant sees a small life-form with the spirit to branch off from the approved path, it rears back and gives a trumpet of satisfaction, right? Wrong.

Any elephant worthy of its peanuts will stamp on those who do not listen to it and obey. It will stamp upon them with its elephant feet and grind them into the dust and dance upon the dust until the memory of those who have been trampled has passed away like the light in the forest.

But as there are many ways to obey, there are also alternatives for those who seek to disobey. And just as Right Obedience must be learned, the art of Right Disobedience must be acquired if we are to continue on our chosen path to leveraging the creature we serve.

BUDDHA BULLETS

THE THREE-LEGGED STOOL OF DISOBEYING

These are powerful tools! Use them wisely or not at all!

◇ **WRONG OBEYING:** This is accomplished by the time-honored methods of Purposeful Misunderstanding and Bad Listening. Both should come naturally to you by now. By pursuing both, you may attain Wrong Obeying. An example: The elephant has told you to fire someone of great value because that person did not polish his toenails with distinction that morning. Instead of firing that person, who is a decent human being and has a family that relies on his earnings, you move the person's desk to a part of the office out of the elephant's view. Later, when the elephant sees the person, as of course it will, it may have forgotten its original order altogether. If it has not and says, "I told you to get that person out of here!" you may then reply, with honesty, "But, my lord! I did. I moved her from over there . . . to over here!" If the elephant is not mollified, one may move on to other methods or stick with this one. There are all kinds of ways to misunderstand a busy elephant or to accomplish the wrong things very, very well indeed.

◇ *PESTERING DISPUTATION:* Elephants hate to talk about their orders. They want only to see them accomplished. One may therefore get the better of any elephant by discussing its orders until the creature's attention span has snapped or its desire to pursue the matter has expired. This is a delicate process and must be done carefully, with infinite regard for the elephant's feelings and great regret for one's inability to understand the how and wherefore of the order that is to be accomplished. "But, my lord," you must say, over and over, "last week you said this was to be done . . . and now you say that something else entirely is to be done. How am I to reconcile those two matters?" Or perhaps: "This is most wonderful, my lord! But how am I to accomplish that if the budget for such things has been assigned to Koplowitz and his people? Shall I call Koplowitz and ask him to appear for a further review of his operating initiatives?" And so forth. While disputing with the elephant, be careful never to roll over into disagreeing with the elephant. Elephant's don't mind disputing. But they hate disagreeing. The rare elephant that brooks extensive disagreeing is probably not an elephant at all, but a gnu in elephant's clothing.

⟡ *NONOBEYING:* The most difficult strategy of all, and available only to extremely dedicated Zen masters. One simply meets the order with Nothingness. No argument. No disputation. No action. No inaction. Thus did Mr. Bartleby, in the story by Herman Melville, confound his superior. "I would prefer not to," he said, then followed up on his preference. Times have moved on since then, and at this point one may not even be safe expressing a preference. You may receive the order. You may, as it were, stare back at the order. Then you may go elsewhere and do other things and, by so doing, Not Do the thing that is to be done. If asked whether it is done, you may reply, "Not yet." This is true and essentially nonconfrontational. When asked why it is not done, you may reply with truth, "I have been doing other things." If asked when it will be done, you may say without prevarication, "As soon as possible, my lord." Your lord, of course, does not know that you find the doing of the thing impossible, so there will be no problem with this as an answer qua answer. And so time will pass. And the thing will not be done. And you will still be alive, and so will the elephant, who you may be sure will eventually arrive at the point where it does not remember what was to be done, why it was to be done, and why an otherwise obedient and excellent handler such as yourself has not seen to its doing. And in the end, my little sprite, it will go away, as all things must, including ourselves, the elephant, and the cosmic infrastructure in which we all reside.

COMPLIMENTING THE ELEPHANT:
LEVEL TWO

To him who constantly practices reverence and respects
the aged, four things will increase: life, beauty,
happiness, and strength.

THE DHAMMAPADA

Wherever the light makes me look best.

*RALPH LAUREN, TO A FORTUNE REPORTER
WHO ASKED HIM WHERE HE'D LIKE
TO SIT FOR AN INTERVIEW*

Ralph Lauren seeks the light that makes him look the
best. It is our task to find that light for our elephant and
place him in it. That is the higher level of complimenting that reaches into the elephant's soul and tickles it in
the best possible way. Happily, you are now ready to do
just that.

Beginners, of course, always babble on about sucking
up and think they know what they are talking about. But
they do not understand the complexity, the many-
faceted beauty of the art itself. They are satisfied with
superficial acts of flattery, simply complimenting the elephant on the length of its tusks, for instance, or the
attractiveness of its studded collar. And certainly, it is the
rare, rare beast that is not susceptible to a little common
grease now and then.

But sucking up, kissing up, brownnosing, and other elementary forms of elephantine ego stimulation are only the starting point for the accomplished handler working to eliminate the weight of an entire elephant. These forms of behavior, as valuable as they may be, are but shallow things, as the Buddha observed one afternoon while waiting in the Pittsburgh airport for a flight back to New York after US Airways once again inexplicably canceled his flight due to "equipment trouble."

KNOW HOW THE ELEPHANT VIEWS ITSELF

In Bill Gates's high-tech Xanadu of a home in Seattle, the library has a dome, and around the base of that dome is this inscription: "He had come a long way to this blue lawn and his dream must have seemed so close he could hardly fail to grasp it." The quotation is from *The Great Gatsby*, F. Scott Fitzgerald's meditation on the self-invented man and the American dream. Though the literary soul shudders at such a notion, Gates sees himself as a Gatsby figure, self-made, fabulously rich, romantic.

The Atlanta Constitution
January 14, 2001

"Simple ingratiation," said the Buddha, without a hint of annoyance that would have been quite normal under the circumstances, "is like lobbing a ripe, delicious fruit through the open window of the elephant's office. The fruit may be appreciated, but it still comes from the outside in. Our goal now is to work from the inside out."

How, then, does one work from the inside out in complimenting the elephant? By taking control of the elephant's environment and shaping the events and situations in such a way that the elephant feels good about itself. In Level One, for example, we might compliment the elephant on its lovely hair. In Level Two, we are bound to improve the elephant's hair to the supermodel status. Anyone thinking this is impossible has never stood up close to Donald Trump when he was with one of his girlfriends.

BUDDHA BULLETS

◆ You have moved from commenting on a fictional reality to creating it.

◆ Creating your own reality in which other people must live is the essence of Buddha.

◆ One may make the universe because it does not exist in any empirical sense. Why may not you construct a reality as well as the next person?

*I can just tell the way people are talking about something that it's
not right. They don't even know it's not right, but I know.*

MEG WHITMAN, CEO, EBAY

I have demonstrated an ability to pick up quickly on the
essence of what's important. I know what I don't know.
And I know that our strengths are complmentary . . . I
bring strategic vision.

CARLY FIORINA, TRYING TO CONVINCE THE HEWLETT-PACKARD
DIRECTORS WHY SHE SHOULD BE CEO

What does one give a creature who knows everything
about everything? How does one import knowledge and
insight into a brain that thinks it invented wisdom?

Perhaps most important to us, little squab, is this:
What kind of control can one establish over a mind that
one has *not,* to some extent, influenced, shaped—even
created? And yet is that mind not impervious to influence?

What is to be done?

The key is to pour a special material into the elephant's mind—one that cannot be found in there without your intervention—and to provide it in such a way
that:

- The elephant believes it was in there already and that it has, in fact, discovered it.
- The elephant becomes excited about the new material it has discovered in its brain and immediately seeks to explore and act upon it.
- Still, in spite of its narcissism, the elephant, in some small corner of its mind, recognizes that it came upon/invented this new knowledge while it was in your presence and associates you with this enhanced awareness of its own splendor.

The elephant knows more about certain things than you do. Their numbers are legion. But there is at least one thing about which it knows nothing, a topic so alien to its makeup that you must provide it. This turf, and this turf alone, provides fit and fertile grounds for its mandatory education.

Things the elephant knows more about than you do	Things that you know more about than the elephant does
What it wants	How other people feel
What it doesn't want	
Its hobbies	
Business	
Specifics of each operating unit	
Wine	
Cheese	
Sailboats	
Crushing enemies/friends	

Yes, the one matter about which it is worth educating the elephant, the one thing you inherently know more about, is *how other people feel*. It is therefore your job, as its handler, to educate the elephant on the subject of Humanity.

An elephant who has no such knowledge is a lost beast whose ruin will attend upon it far sooner than you would like. To succeed, there must be some glimmer of knowledge about people. And since it is not a person, it needs your help.

You must introduce the notions, feelings, and realities of humankind in such a way that the elephant believes it has discovered this trove itself. Eventually, you must enable the elephant to convert this new understanding into management that makes the lives of others in its service more tolerable.

BUDDHA BULLETS

○ Talk to the elephant about other people's feelings. Do not tell. Mention. Suggest. Imply.

○ It may be possible at first that the elephant has no idea that other people do have feelings. It may be possible that it doesn't recognize that there are other people.

○ Praise the elephant when it responds to the humanity of others. Make it feel good about itself when it is guided by the feelings of others.

○ Be quietly censorious when the elephant fails to perform well in this regard. But do not blame it. It is merely being itself.

- Be patient. Keep at it. Be light of touch and sleight of hand. It may take years. But if it pays off in an elephant even slightly more aware of others as a consideration in its life, you have done your job. And doing your job is dharma.

- Obviously, in the end, you will be the laboratory in which the elephant tries any new "humanity" it might discover in itself. Encourage its early stumbling efforts, even when they slightly trample or crunch you in uncomfortable ways. For when the elephant has succeeded with you, it may move on to others in the wider world . . . and take you with it as its tutor, guide, and companion.

The trial probably was lost in Gates' videotaped deposition, dolloped by [David Boies] piecemeal throughout the proceedings. Rocking in his chair, reflexively sipping a soft drink, the famously competitive Gates petulantly dodged questions while claiming he was motivated solely by his desire to serve customers and to save Microsoft from impending doom.

CHICAGO TRIBUNE
JANUARY 14, 2001

Throughout the proceedings against it, Microsoft behaved characteristically true to form. It was always, in its own eyes, the underdog, beset at both the left and the right by unjust campaigns against it. It never veered from its stance that it had never leaned its enormous gray body against the rest of the industry in a daily, quite public attempt to roll over on top of its competitors and crush them. That was its legal position, and it stuck to it.

For years leading up to the trial, the elephant behaved in a similarly consistent style. It terrorized its rivals. If there was a competitor it could not trample, it would pick it up in its giant trunk, shake it violently, and eat it. That was its competitive position, and it stuck to it.

And eventually, because no alternatives were presented to it, the elephant was fated to end up where it did—in court, with a public, a judge, and the full weight of the media machine arrayed against it. And the best testimony against it was the videotaped deposition of the elephant who ran the show. In his testimony, Bill Gatsby went confidently forth, telling the video camera exactly what he'd been saying to everybody around him for years without visible contradiction. Why would he doubt himself? Was his way not the One Way?

It is now fairly clear that there was some teleological gap in Redmond, Washington, where the Microsoft elephant pen is located. Programmers they have enough. Marketers and public relations people and human resources professionals and a craven team of yes-man lawyers and a legion of impressive executives in aggressively open collars bred to lead a whole infrastructure designed and built to bestride the digital world like a Colossus, they have it all.

But no elephant handlers. If there had been elephant handlers anywhere in the village, would not one have raised his slender, crooked stick to the eye of the elephant and said, "Ho! Jumbo! Do not crush that mouse for it may have attorneys of its own!"

No such stick was raised. No such voice was heard. Yes, there was much macho posturing, we may be sure, much heat in telling the elephant what it most wanted to hear, much chuckling about the last little rodent whose bones snapped under the weight of the beast. But sadly, no still, small voice crying in the wilderness.

Those who surrounded Bill Gates did him no service. They got a lot of stock options, though, and that is something.

To be a compleat handler, one must know how to raise that voice from the heart of what is indeed Nothingness. In that hostile, empty land lies a range of alternatives on all subjects of interest to the elephant. But no one will see them until one comes to look for them and turns the frozen landscape into a splendid garden. That one is you, Zen pupil, Zen master.

Like any task, the presentation of alternatives takes preparation, but in the end it must honestly be embraced and accomplished. It is part of your job. Do it. In this case, doing nothing produces nothing but more nothing. Doing something is sometimes better than doing nothing, even Zen-wise. This is one of those times.

BUDDHA BULLETS

ON PRESENTING ALTERNATIVES

○ *STEP ONE:* Recognize that there are alternatives. For all but the most mature elephants, this in itself is a revolutionary concept. If you have spent a great deal of time with such an elephant, you yourself may have trouble believing in the possibility of alternative points of view.

For you to see the alternatives, you must train yourself to stand outside the prevailing culture and look in upon it as it chuckles along in all its maniacal self-satisfaction. Remember! You are not of it. You are around and inside and above and beneath it. But it is not a part of you and you are not a part of it because there is no It and there is no You. There is only Everything. At one with that Everything, you may see the true nature of It All, how it is working, and how it might otherwise work if a questioning mind was brought to its operations.

⟡ *STEP TWO:* Know the alternatives. Study the situation as one would an orange, looking at all sides and angles, from top to bottom. How many sides are there to an object that has none? How many angles are there to an object that has none? An infinite number, right?

⟡ *STEP THREE:* Communicate the alternatives. How? You know how. In its infinite wisdom, did not the eternal cosmos create ample meetings? Are there not moments when the elephant looks about itself and pretends to ask for strategic counsel? Of course there are. The issue is not one of opportunity, little weasel, but of courage. Remember courage?

Be not loud. Be not shrill. You are not presenting advice. You are merely laying out differing scenarios to those that are accepted as common wisdom. Others will look at you as if you had just sprouted a second head. But that is all right. They are not the handlers. You are. And as for courage:

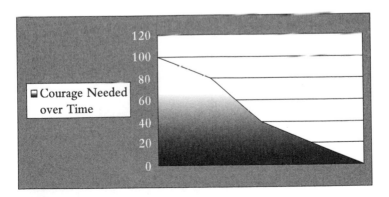

It is always hardest to jump into the deep end of the pool the first time you try. When one is used to the water, it becomes fun.

"Look!" people will say. "Look at how well that fellow swims!"

Convincing the Elephant That It Was the Elephant's Idea

I'm not going to stick around to save the world.

JOHN REED AT A CITIGROUP BOARD MEETING AT WHICH
HE LOST A BATTLE WITH CO-CEO SANDY WEILL
AND WAS FORCED TO RETIRE

As it is written: A young Internet monk was hungry one afternoon and searched about for a place to grab a bite to eat. He went into an obviously fancy place at which patrons had to wear not only a tie but a sport coat as well. Being a budding executive in a failing dotcom concern, he owned neither and was dressed in the mandatory outfit of his generation—baggy white shirt, jeans, and moccasins without socks. "You will need appropriate luncheon attire to eat here, sir," said the maître d' of the establishment, who retained more power and personal prestige in the business community than did many CEOs. "Well," said the monk, departing the restaurant with some noise and even a little heat, "I wouldn't be seen dead in this place anyway!"

Indeed, as the Buddha himself said to his disciples when they were all trying to figure out where to sit for disputation that evening, "It is easy to heap condemnation on an establishment at which one may not expect a very good table."

This ability to render misfortune and rejection into a

positive act initiated by oneself is the property of all great elephants. And it represents a tremendous boon to its handlers. Any situation, no matter how dire, can be transformed into a positive reality once the elephant is made to understand its necessity. Once it is inevitable, the elephant may easily be made to see that it is *exactly as elephant itself would have wished.*

This is easy when the thing to be bogusly owned by the elephant is positive. The sutra is most useful, however, when the matter is of possible negative import. That is the subject of which we will deal in the next chapter, and a dangerous topic it is to those who do not know how to turn the elephant on its pointy little tail.

BUDDHA BULLETS

- ⟨⟩ It is in the elephant's nature to see all things as creations and extensions of itself. You are therefore doing nothing in this regard but validating the elephant's true self.

- ⟨⟩ To the elephant, if a thing is happening, then it is of the elephant's doing in some way or other, or the elephant has much it can do to turn the matter to its advantage.

- ⟨⟩ This may seem nonsensical, but it is no more nonsensical than anything else in a universe that is, in its essence, neither real nor unreal.

- ⟨⟩ In short, why not?

INFORMING THE ELEPHANT OF BAD NEWS

I don't think he's very smart. . . . He's the general counsel
of this company. He should have said . . . "Look, you guys
can't do this. Now is the time to be flexible."

*JUDGE THOMAS PENFIELD JACKSON, ASSESSING LEAD
MICROSOFT ATTORNEY BILL NEUKOM'S INABILITY TO
PERSUADE EXECUTIVES TO ALTER THEIR "HARD-CORE" STANCE*

Scared money never wins.

ANONYMOUS

As we have noted in our wisdom . . . it would have
made sense, would it not? For someone to have
approached Mr. Gatsby and told him that things weren't
going very well with the judge? Incredibly, no one in
the entire organization was willing to do that job. No
one to deliver bad news.

Just think what might have happened to Microsoft as
a result . . . had not a Republican administration been
elected and all antitrust considerations been therefore
consigned to oblivion.

It takes no courage to give the elephant good news.
Nowhere in the Buddha's business thought is there a
teaching on that subject. "He who cannot safely present
good news has eaten the fruit of the Doofus Tree," said
the Buddha, then moved on to more difficult subjects.

But bad news is something else, because someone must be blamed for bad news.

If there is someone logical who may be blamed, that is very well and good, and most sane elephants will cast about for the one most responsible for the bad news. But in situations of unclarity, or when the bad news involves many people, or a group diffuse and geographically far-flung . . . well, then, the entity that must be blamed is the one who had the bad taste, temerity, and faulty wisdom to bring the news itself.

This is called Shooting the Messenger, and it is not a game. An elephant can punish in several ways the person who presents it with bad news:

- One can be trampled outright.
- One can be left standing in limbo for a time while the elephant circles the area in rage, then be skewered by an angry tusk from behind.
- One can be picked up and thrown into a solid object.
- One can be dismissed coldly, then ignored at bonus time.
- In rare and dramatic cases, one can be eaten. For while preferring vegetables and grasses, a significant number of business elephants have turned their back upon nature and are, in fact, carnivores. And a carnivorous elephant is a very scary concept indeed.

To avoid these fates, present bad news to the elephant in this fashion:

1 Position yourself immediately beneath the most heavy portion of the elephant.

2 Curl yourself into as small a physical presence as possible.

3 Lean into the elephant, so that the greater part of the elephant's weight is now leaning over you at an angle.

4 Make a sharp movement toward the elephant while offering the piece of bad news. This double action should serve to make the elephant top-heavy to the point of actually falling over.

5 As the elephant falls over, rush forward and beneath its body as it flips upward, assuring that when it does right itself on its own, you will be found *on the other side of the elephant entirely.* At advanced levels, you will be able to spin the elephant into the proper position, but at this point you should be satisfied simply to use the ridiculous disparity in your body weights against it.

6 As the elephant attempts to digest the bad news—and this is absolutely crucial—offer it another tidbit immediately, as one would offer a choking friar a small piece of rye bread to settle his gorge. This morsel might pertain to the bad news—a possible culprit who could be blamed, other than yourself?—or be a completely different scary thing entirely. The goal is to make the elephant get its trunk around something different from the all-consuming bad thing itself.

The better part of valor is discretion.

WILLIAM SHAKESPEARE

Of course, if the bad thing is very big and very bad, one might consider having someone else do it.

BUDDHA BULLET

◌ As the Buddha said one afternoon on the twelfth hole of the Bel Air Country Club, immediately prior to what looked to be a serious thunderstorm, "When lightning is obviously about to strike a certain tree, one must consider sitting under another."

There's never been a single meeting where an executive represented his or her interests or those of his or her department over the interests of the company. If that happened, I'd probably end the meeeting.

TOM SIEBEL, CHAIRMAN AND CEO
SIEBEL SYSTEMS

Amazing. Your average elephant believes that kind of nonsense, while pursuing his own interests (which are, in his imagination, one with the company's) relentlessly and inexorably every day. And you must work within that belief system or die in the attempt to escape from it.

In this worldview, you are not working for you. You are working, depending on the nature of your elephant, for:

- The good of the elephant
- The good of the shareholders
- The good of mankind
- The good of the team
- The death of the other guy

The one thing you are not working for, then, is credit for yourself. You may therefore never ask for personal credit for yourself. As it is written, "He who asks for personal credit for him- or herself deserves a quick paperweight in the back of head from everyone who feels they have earned a portion of glory for that which has been done."

> *Wherever you go,*
> *there you are.*
> ANONYMOUS

So don't ask for credit. Simply make sure that you find yourself in its path as it is apportioned. "Location, location, location," saith the scribes, and they're not simply speaking of real estate. You need to be at the right place at the right time to get into the line of positive fire.

You can best ensure that position by being the one to offer the last scrap of work to the elephant when the job in question is nearing completion.

The final draft of the document . . .

The last iteration of the contract . . .

The moment when the new spreadsheet application is being launched on the elephant's desktop for the first time (as long as it works) . . .

The hour when the bottle of bubbly is brought in for popping, the Lucite tombstone commemorating the deal is presented to senior management, the very end of the final conference call when the Release button is pushed on the speakerphone and a general murmur of closure encircles the room . . .

The great and fallen Siddhartha of popular culture, Allen Stewart Konigsberg, has said, and it is true in spite of his compromised standing, "Eighty percent of success is showing up."

Be there. Or be Nowhere.

◇ There will be those who seek to bar you from the room when credit is about to flow. Such people are not your friends.

◇ Carry a small, metaphysical letter opener about your person at all times. Be prepared to use it. Sometimes it is necessary to face the void with a weapon in one's hand. To do less is to deny one's essential nature and the structure of All That Is.

◇ Just because you are a child of Zen does not require you to be a schmuck. *Au contraire.* Fight for your standing in the great mandala of credit for things well done. You'll be glad you did.

I'm a religious man. I pray for Milky Way.
I pray for Snickers.

FORREST MARS SR.
FOUNDER, MARS INC.

Which is presumably why people keep eating them candy bars.

Understand: the elephant may do no work at all, but that is not the way it perceives things.

Instead, it believes everything that goes on within the confines of the company is, to some greater or lesser extent, a portion of his or her manifest destiny, the cosmic fix that is in to make things work out for it personally. What it does not do, Brahma has done for it, because as we know, Brahma has nothing to do but lob in assistance for the elephant, with whom He is well pleased.

It is therefore impossible to find anything that is done in the ecosystem of your company that the elephant does not feel in some way is its doing, and for which it is not justified in receiving praise.

Here is a truly stunning trick that will prove the truth of this concept.

Approach the elephant's assistant. Suggest that the assistant purchase something for the elephant's office—a vase with flowers or a new scissors and letter-opener set.

Wait for the object to be placed within the elephant's pen. Then enter that enclosure and compliment the elephant on its good taste. By far most elephants will accept the compliment without indicating that they had nothing to do with the acquisition whatsoever.

The same holds true for business actions, thoughts, and accomplishments. It is the very, very rare elephant indeed that will not feel gratified and accept all kinds of congratulations for things it did not do. Most remarkably, after the second or third round of such congratulations, the elephant will begin to forget it did not do the thing in question, will take ownership of it, and feel proud of itself for having done it.

Several years ago, the Buddha sat beneath the tree of a certain great elephant warlord. This warlord spent most of his time pacing his office, eating soup and breadsticks and plotting the invasion and conquest of a neighboring kingdom. To accomplish this great task, he approached the elephants that ran the empire of which his province was a part. "We must conquer the Nordlingers!" he exhorted. At first, they were reticent. Then they came to believe. One night, they came in, trampled over the little warlord's kraal, and threw him off a cliff. Then they went forth and conquered the Nordlingers.

Several years later, the Buddha found himself under a tree with one of these great and triumphant beasts that had destroyed his little warlord. "One of my favorite memories is the conquest of the Nordlingers," said the big and still quite dangerous elephant. "It was hard work, but once I get an idea in my head, nothing stops me." The Buddha said nothing, for saying nothing was the Buddha's specialty and one of the reasons he lived to such an advanced age in spite of his weight and his sedentary lifestyle.

◇ The elephant believes it created the world around it and controls everything about that world.

◇ Offering credit for that which it did not do is simply another way of verifying that irrational conceit.

◇ One may at times provide a light in which the elephant may bask.

◇ There is no danger that the elephant will resent the light.

Having a Nice, No-Agenda Chat
with the Elephant

I figure that no matter what I am doing,
I'd better do it well.

*Meg Whitman, CEO of eBay, during a photo shoot for
the cover of a business magazine in which she was
made to kneel with her chin on a table littered with
PEZ dispensers for half an hour*

Time is money.

Anonymous

Elephants even waste time better than others do. You
can help. Your right to hobnob aimlessly with the elephant is determined to a large extent by your size,
might, and economic impact within the body of the
corporation . . . but not as directly as you might think.
Viz:

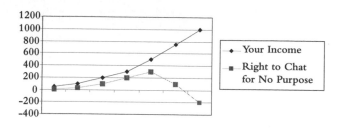

Things that can be accomplished in a no-agenda chat with the elephant:

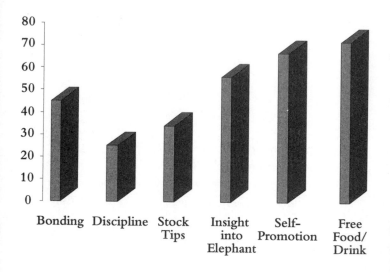

Topics that may be discussed in a no-agenda chat with the elephant:

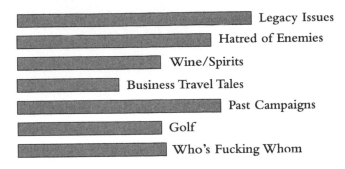

Legacy Issues

Hatred of Enemies

Wine/Spirits

Business Travel Tales

Past Campaigns

Golf

Who's Fucking Whom

Who should set the agenda of topics during your no-agenda chat with the elephant:

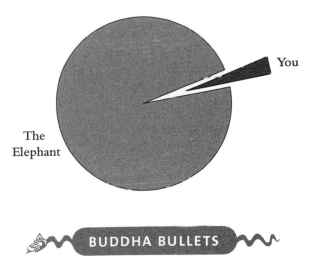

You

The
Elephant

BUDDHA BULLETS

- Do not be too quick to rush into the silence. The elephant enjoys listening to itself think and wants you to listen, too.

- If you have an agenda, leave it at the door. You are on the elephant's time.

When You and the Elephant Are out of Town

Amid the restructuring, the *Exxon Valdez* ran aground in 1989. Lee Raymond, who was Exxon president at the time, was dispatched to oversee the cleanup and the immense fallout. He was so faceless that he once walked into an office in Alaska to file a claim, posing as a Valdez resident, so he could assess the claims process.

WALL STREET JOURNAL
DECEMBER 1, 1999

People are strange, when you're a stranger.

THE DOORS

It is a common experience. You meet a person in the daily run of business. You come to know him well. Then one day you see him at the local mall, or on the street in another city, and he is a complete stranger to you.

Context is all.

When an elephant moves out of town, away from its home compound and customary haunts, it loses a small and recognizable piece of its elephant nature and becomes, in its own way, more human, and less recognizable not only to its handlers, but also to itself.

The road is a delicate place for your elephant, and both a challenge and an opportunity for you, its guide and servant. Here is a quick guide to help you on your path.

The opportunities for intimacy and enjoyment are

Elephant
Out-of-Town Behavior

Elephant Action	Positive Implications	Negative Implications	Potential Response
Gets drunk	Intimacy	Shame and recrimination/ witnesses must be eliminated	Drink along for a time, then go to room
Stays out too late	Friendship	Show too much of you, see too much of it	Hang around in increasing silence, then go to room
Screws up business transaction due to lack of context	Elephant vulnerability gives you opening for counsel/advice	Elephant must execute anyone who saw its vulnerability	Go to room as soon as possible
Elephant eats unwisely	Fun with elephant	Elephant associates you with nausea	Get sicker than elephant, more publicly, taking anecdotal burden on yourself
Tries to have sex with inappropriate animal	Hard to determine	Total disaster for everybody	Go to room, check out of hotel, leave town

many . . . and the perils associated with such opportunities are as prodigious as the elephant's appetites.

For it is on the road when most elephants lose their equilibrium and need the greatest external control. They drink. They smoke. They try to pick up emus and gazelles for a stroll around the swimming pool. When they can, they gamble. They lose their sense of who they are.

You must remind them. Be gentle . . . an accomplice, if you choose to be. But never forget that the elephant is not your friend. It is not your buddy. It is still and always the elephant.

Management of the beast is best, of course. But just as there come times to Be There, there are also times when it is best to embrace the void, slip into it quietly, and be . . . Not.

BUDDHA BULLETS

○ When the elephant finds a couple of girls who will do anything it wants for only $50, it is possible that the time has come to be . . . Not.

○ When the elephant is leering over the senior vice president of human resources, who is equally drunk and has long, long legs and very red hair, it is possible that the time has come to be . . . Not.

○ When the elephant must be carried back to its room between two grown men who love it and can't stand to see it passed out in their arms, it is possible that, once the elephant is deposited in its straw, the time has come to be . . . Not.

But:

○ When the elephant is standing in the lobby of the hotel, clearly between things, unattended, swaying back and forth like a lost calf, it is possible that the time has come to . . . be There.

○ When the elephant has had no dinner, but has been so obsessed with greeting people or gambling at the $50 table or munching on breadsticks and olives in the bar that it has done nothing about substantially feeding itself . . . be There.

◌ When the elephant's deal has fallen apart and for the moment it is at a loss for words . . .

◌ When the elephant asks you to fly back with it on its G5 for no particular reason . . .

◌ When the elephant is sitting in an office someplace away from home, its right hand on the steel desk and its left hand twiddling its fingers in its enormous lap . . .

Be there when you should be there. And be Not when you should Not.

In knowing the difference, there is Buddha. And opportunities for promotion, too.

GETTING DRUNK WITH THE ELEPHANT

There was clearly alcohol involved.

A BUSINESS COLLEAGUE ON THOMAS M. HAYTHE,
PARTNER, LAW FIRM HAYTHE & CURLEY, AFTER
HAYTHE WAS FORCED TO RESIGN FROM HIS OWN
FIRM AFTER "INAPPROPRIATE" BEHAVIOR AT A
CELEBRATORY SOCIAL EVENING

At a party celebrating the acquisition of Salomon Smith
Barney, Sandy Weill and protégé/heir-apparent Jamie
Dimon sat down to drinks and started to argue about a
seemingly trivial detail. Within moments they were
screaming at each other.

NEW YORK TIMES MAGAZINE
AUGUST 27, 2000

Which is your elephant?

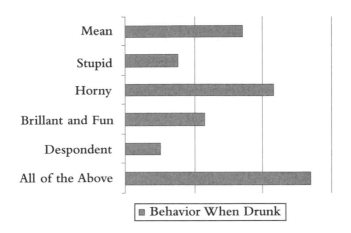

Mean	
Stupid	
Horny	
Brillant and Fun	
Despondent	
All of the Above	

Behavior When Drunk

This multiplicity of big behavior, which is only aggravated with the introduction of alcohol, may be broken down into the following for the vast majority of elephants:

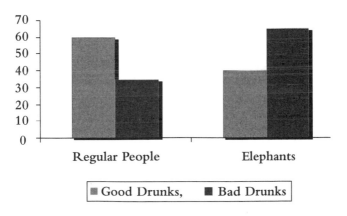

Good Drunks,   Bad Drunks

This means several things to you, little mosquito on the great interstate of life:

- It means one may at times be required to take in liquor with the elephant.
- It means one may watch as the elephant becomes increasingly inebriated and enjoy the feeling of proximity to the great beast as it is unwinding.
- It means one may be gratified while observing the elephant becoming more sodden and excessive, up to a point.
- But one may never oneself become drunk while drinking with the elephant. That is the heart of the sutra. If you cannot learn it, go off and drink with vice presidents for the rest of your life.

As the Buddha said while watching the great multiplicity of existence play out before his eyes at the Four Seasons bar in New York City: "One must always be two drinks behind the elephant."

Two drinks behind. Consider that.

So while the elephant is railing about its adversaries, a dangerous glint in its eye, you may be relaxed and well lubricated, certainly, but not in a condition where it is conceivable to stand up on your legs and shout at high volume, "We're gonna fuck those bastards!"

And while the elephant is confiding in you, its breath close to your ear, imparting feelings and information that might not be appropriate in the light of day, it is probably best that you not be in a condition where the impulse rises to give the elephant a slobby kiss upon its metaphysical cheek.

And when the elephant tells you what it really, really thinks . . . you must not be in a condition to do the same without the customary filtration systems between your mind and your mouth.

And when the elephant wants to fight with an NFL linebacker who supposedly shoved it, you must be ready to escort it upstairs, not to throw the second punch.

And when the elephant wants to go to the strip club that feeds a report of its visitors to the gossip page of the newspaper the next day, you must be in a position to advise against such a course and not to say "Yuparoonies!"

And when the elephant gets sick and must be carried somewhere for its own comfort, you must be capable of doing so, not to need such humiliating transportation yourself.

And if the elephant should happen to lose its car keys in its own best interest, and they should happen to fall into your hands, oh, merry handler, it is advisable that you not be in a state that you inadvertently kill the elephant on a hairpin curve going ninety while you both are singing "Wooly Bully."

But talk? Laugh? Compare notes? Have good, clean, wholesome, loopy, and somewhat interpersonal fun? That is the way of the ancients who achieved wisdom, and probably how they achieved it.

BUDDHA BULLETS

On Drunkenness

○ The elephant may get drunk. You may not. You may drink. But you may not lose sight of dharma.

- As always, know your elephant. Some cannot drink and maintain elephant dignity. If you are present when elephant dignity is lost, you too will be lost.

- Elephants who drink Scotch will tend to achieve a mellow status more quickly and evenly than those who drink vodka and gin. Clear spirits destroy karma. Brown spirits build karma.

- Wine without food makes elephants stupid.

On Elephant Humor

One morning I shot an elephant in my pajamas. How he
got into my pajamas I'll never know.

GROUCHO MARX

God appeared to us in the guise of Walter Chrysler, and
he offered to buy the Dodge Company.

FERDINAND EBERSTADT, PARTNER, DILLION READ,
ON THE STOCK MANEUVER THAT SWUNG CONTROL
OF DODGE TO CHRYSLER

Humor is incongruity in action. The universe is incon-
gruous. Humor is therefore the best expression of the
truth underlying the universe. It is, in its very essence,
the heart of Zen.

Business is serious. One must believe that business is
essentially serious in order to be good at it. And yet, as
we have said, the universe is not serious. We may therefore understand that business is therefore the best expression of the layer of illusion that overlies the reality of the
teeming, cosmic void that is the universe.

Humor is reality. Business is illusion.

Har har hardy har har.

JACKIE GLEASON

In the disparity between the seriousness of everyday business life and the underlying emptiness and arbitrariness of existence, the discrepancy between the self-importance and stupefying sobriety of business and the inherent frivolity and infinite smallness of all human activity in the face of the infinite, there is laughter.

In that gap between what is Zen and what is no-Zen lies a tremendous garden in which humor can and must thrive.

He or she who can make the elephant laugh holds the fulcrum of power in hand.

The problem is, most elephants, indeed most creatures no matter their size, do not possess an inherent sense of humor. What the average elephant regards as amusing, isn't.

The good news is that one does not have to be particularly funny to make the elephant laugh. The *attempt to provide amusement* is more important than the quality or validity of the amusement itself.

To be a reliable source of amusement, one must simply be:

- Impeccable at the work, so as to not be classified simply as a buffoon.
- Courageously silly when the opportunity presents itself, giving the elephant a small peek at the Zen core of unseriousness that underlies the illusory shell of the world as the elephant has defined it.
- Learn a few jokes.

In themselves, elephants are rarely amusing. It is the rare elephant that is funny in person, although there are some. The Buddha himself once worked for an elephant that kept everyone laughing while in the midst of the most serious business imaginable, but the Buddha has noted that such is the exception that proved the rule. Most elephants are impressed by the seriousness of their mission and the gravitas of the amazing tale of their existence, and one must be careful in puncturing that illusion lest the elephant find the flip side of laughter, which is anger.

That trip is easily made, by the way, since many elephants find as much amusement in cruelty as they do in humor. Around those kinds of beasts, it is best to be wary and to confine oneself to the lowest forms of benign humor: well-tested jokes and the occasional barb of sarcasm against a recognized enemy or foe. Those with a bit more latitude may begin by recognizing that the very tools one uses in business hold a capacity for humor. The same charting program that gives you this . . .

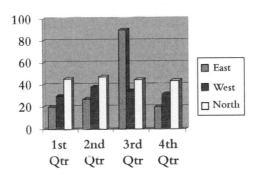

. . . can also be used to provide this:

Inappropriate Words at a Business Meeting

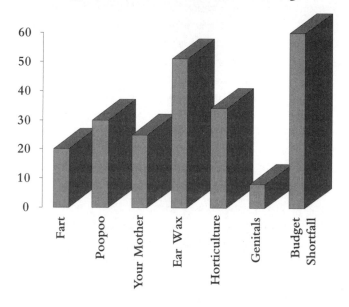

Props may be used, of course. Funny hats, fruit, whatever is at hand.

The best humor is always improvised. The key is this: if you think it is funny, it probably is. So try. The worst you can do is bomb. And the effort is not unappreciated by an elephant that even slightly loves you.

One final concept of overarching import must be mentioned as part of your Duty. In business, one must always Present a Laughing Front to jokes and "amusing" witticisms offered by the elephant itself.

There was once a young bodhisattva who believed it was in the nature of his quest for truth to decline laughter at the humor of the elephant in his charge. "How will the elephant respect me and follow my guidance if it believes me to be an insincere, grinning hypocrite laughing at that which I find not funny?" he asked. Time after time this honest elephant evinced this laudable commitment to virtue. Perhaps the fifteenth time he failed to evince any amusement at an obviously appropriate moment, the elephant made a loud noise and stepped on his head, sending the larger part of his brain matter leaping from his ears and out onto the conference table around which they were meeting. Those who were present say that the sight was not without inherent humor. People laughed, in any event.

BUDDHA BULLETS

SUBJECTS FOR ELEPHANT HUMOR

◇ *GOLF:* It is hilarious when a golf ball is launched from a tee and lands in an unexpected location!

◇ *INAPPROPRIATE SOCIAL BEHAVIOR IN OTHER PEOPLE:* It is equally amusing when an otherwise dignified person commits a gaffe that embarrasses him and everyone around him!

◇ *FAILURE OF ADVERSARIES:* Did you hear the one about the guy at the competing company who got fired? It's a riot!

◇ *BAD THINGS/GREAT THINGS/AMAZING THINGS THE ELEPHANT HAS DONE:* Remember the time the elephant bowled a 300? Stole that little investment banking company out from under Lenny Lerner?

Took the keys to the Hummer and threw them in the lake? It's to laugh!

○ *INFANTILE DIRTY JOKES:* Did you hear the one about the girl who bent over and showed her bottom? Ha!

○ *DEMOCRATS WHO HAVE SEX WITH PEOPLE:* Bill Clinton is gone. But the wonderful humor of the years when the Republican Congress spoiled his administration are not forgotten. Nota bene: On the other hand, stories about Republicans who visit their desperately ill wives in the hospital in order to break up with them are part of the liberal media bias.

○ Hillary Clinton, on the other hand—now that's funny!

PLAYING GOLF WITH THE ELEPHANT

A mind is a terrible thing to waste.

UNCF SLOGAN

Business Effectiveness as a Function of Time Spent Golfing

- ■ CEO
- ☐ Sales VP
- ■ Total Idiot with Nothing Else to Do

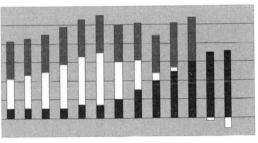

Time Spent Golfing

Golf is the crack cocaine of the ruling class. Those who become addicted live in their own subculture, one in which foolish tales of the game and discussion of associated paraphernalia ultimately destroy otherwise useful lives.

As we can see from the chart above, powerful CEO elephants can maintain their business effectiveness over time, even using the addiction to lend them preternatural strength, but even they reach a point where effectiveness ends and dotage begins. Sales executives too, who often use the golf drug in their line of work, reach a point of diminishing returns. The only category of elephant that benefits from continual golfing is the last on the list, since there even golf can do little to erode nonexistent brain function.

Like all narcotics, golf is dangerous but nonlethal when used recreationally. It is only later, when the addicted elephant builds up a tolerance for it, that we find the poor creature tumbling down the path to senescence and professional drooling.

To handle the golfing elephant, one must understand the ironic problem that is facing it: the better you are at the game, the more frustrating and emotionally destructive it is. It is the endorphin rush that comes with achieving continual failure in spite of striving that is unique and heady to the successful elephant. The worse it does, the more addicted to the experience it becomes.

Therefore, if one is bad at it, one can have fun. Likewise, if one is moderately good and able to control one's expectations of the game, one can still enjoy it a little bit. But if one has any pretensions to ability in the game, it will feast upon one's ego, destroy one's peace of mind, dash one's belief in the possibility of personal improvement, and ultimately erode one's sanity to the breaking point.

Remember: desire is suffering. For all but the truly fortunate, who have come to master the thing itself and thereby achieve Nothingness in it, golf is all about frustrated desire. It is suffering. It is not Zen.

You must, however, live in a world with those who golf. How is this to be done?

There are but two roads open to you. Masterful Play and No Play.

Masterful play is open only to those who are masterful. Are you masterful? Can you hit straight from your mind's eye onto the fairway? When your concentration strays and you err in some way, does it disquiet your mind or does your consciousness remain a still and soothing pond and all that? If you are not masterful, do not strive for mastery while in your cleats. That way lies sadness, madness, and an end to gladness. Find your mastery where it might benefit someone other than yourself and your caddy.

No Play takes three forms.

ALTERNATIVE PLAY: There are tennis and raquetball and squash, for those who like to break a sweat upon their brows. There is even poker, the game of kings. If others are still out swinging their clubs around, there are the sauna and the steam room and possibly even the massage table after an hour or so on the weight machines. There is much you can do to No Play. Men and women have lived their lives without golf and gone on to do wonderful things.

PLAY WITH DUMMIES: There are always those who love the outdoors and do not mind appearing foolish in front of some congenial peers. Buddha loves such people. No Play of this sort cannot be done around elephants, but it is not important for you to be around the elephant when fate has plunged him in the sewage drainpipe.

WORK: Even the most addicted elephant cannot look sideways at a warrior who is seated on the patio with an iced tea and a big stack of spreadsheets. Somewhere in the back of his atrophying mind, even the most addicted golfer knows that somewhere work is going on by men and women who are not golfing at that moment, and that that is good.

Feel no envy for the golfing elephant and those who attend it. Remember: some places it is better not to be. Some things it is better not to do. Life is too short to be engaged in activities that make one wish it were shorter.

BUDDHA BULLETS

GOLF

◇ If your elephant defines itself by golf, and you cannot break your elephant's addiction to golf, and you cannot get it to concentrate on anything that is Not Golf, and you do not wish to spend your life emotionally crumpled into a corner with a nine iron in your fist, babbling about great courses you have seen and amusing events that transpired years before among men who no longer exist in this plane, the time has come to consider that which freezes the blood of any warrior: finding a new elephant.

◇ All elephants move on sooner or later. Golfing elephants go sooner.

FACING THE ANGRY ELEPHANT

Do the top half!

Ex-Emerson CEO Charles F. Knight to a top executive who had asked him which projects he should tackle first. In a rage, Knight tore the list into two pieces and handed it back

Fear is like fire. If you don't know how to handle it, it can kill you. But if you use it correctly, it can warm your house.

Cus D'Amato
Mike Tyson's trainer

Many elephants are docile . . . much of the time. Why should they not be? They receive all the hay they can eat, oblivious to how it was produced and not forced to reach into their trunks to pay for it. They are carefully washed and brushed by armies of little people who wish for nothing more than the privilege of continuing in that function. Nothing that the elephant sees around it displeases it, generally. It has nothing to be angry about, because it controls the universe.

Except that it does not. Constantly every day, and possibly during certain difficult periods, every hour of every day, the elephant is presented with proof that it does not exert control over anything beyond its own little circle of influence.

Every bodhisattva knows: The universe is not under any being's control. Circle within inexorable circle, it moves along grooves of its own devising, not ours. All efforts to control it are and must be futile. Elephant and gnu, spider and dragon, mail room worker and CEO, we are all a part of the great Nothing that is Everything. This is the lesson of the Buddha.

The elephant cannot see this, because it believes that *it* is everything. But as we have seen, it is not everything at all. It is just . . . well, an elephant.

The distance between what the elephant believes itself to be and the actual reality of its true nature will, when presented to the elephant, make it angry.

You can do nothing about this anger, which is often highly flammable and out of proportion to its cause. You can simply keep the elephant company during its times of disappointment and, if possible, reap some benefit from that proximity.

How many are the events that will make the elephant angry!

Occasionally toughness does involve some old-fashioned ass-kicking. There are times, for example, when on the spur of the moment I'll dial the number of one of my hotels or the Trump Shuttle, just to see how long it takes my people to answer the phone. If I have to wait for more than five or six rings, I'll tell the employee who finally does answer who I am. Then I'll ask—without hiding my annoyance— what the problem is. I've found that usually that person will not have to be reminded about the standards I expect.

DONALD TRUMP

Deals will fall through. Members of the opposite sex will fail to perform as required, from first wives who refuse to go away to arm candy that believes itself to be in line for more than it is likely to receive. People will fail to achieve excellence in its service. The store will be out of the elephant's favorite cologne or cigar or shade of lip gloss. The fourth-quarter numbers will be down instead of up, because the elephant cannot control a $4-trillion industry that insists, at least for the time being, on being down 2 percent. It is raining, and the elephant wanted it to be sunny for its drive up to Napa. The soup is cold. The lobster salad is insufficiently chilled. The universe is out of control! Help!

The elephant's anger is its means of reestablishing its illusion of control over its world. Faced with its true nugatoriness in the scheme of things—a status it shares with all of creation—it will instinctively exert itself over its environment and seek to reshape it into a form it will recognize. Anger is often its tool.

There are two kinds of anger you will need to face and master if you are to live long in the elephant's gigantic shadow.

- *Anger #1:* You have erred and caused the elephant pain.
- *Anger #2:* You have done nothing but be present when the elephant is confronted with its true nature.

With luck, you will for the most part find yourself in situation #2. If such is not the case, it is possible that you should be working not for an elephant at all, but for an emu, gazelle, or archaeopteryx.

THE FOUR-TONGUED WHIP OF FOCUSED ATONEMENT

Dealing with the Elephant's Anger
When You Are to Blame

* Breathe deeply. Breath is life.
* Admit your error immediately, with dignity and as little groveling as possible. Some, once they begin a spasm of mandatory groveling, enter into it with fullness of spirit. Resist this temptation. Grovel only as long as you must, then cease groveling. And when you do leave off groveling, do not beat yourself up about having groveled. All of God's creatures have, at one time or another, groveled. The guilt that attends groveling is more debilitating in the end than the groveling itself. He who grovels best grovels light.
  * ✓ *SUPPLEMENTAL BUDDHA BULLETIN:* Do not, however, fall from groveling into cringing! It is impossible to see the sun when your back is bent.
* Promise to fix the source of the elephant's anger right away . . . even if you cannot.
* Get out of the room.

THE SIX-PETALED FLOWER OF BOGUS ATONEMENT

Dealing with the Elephant's Anger
When You Are Not to Blame

- Hear the elephant's blast. There is no pain like elephant pain, because in that pain is the understanding that the world is not conforming to limitless hopes and mountainous dreams. Stand tall, then, in the shadow of its rage. It has nothing to do with you.

- Suffer the injustice. The beast is angry with the universe. You are part of the universe. Why then should it not be angry with you? Accept the anger. You are a representative of the cosmos that has offended the elephant. Feel it burn. It is around you, above you, below you. But it is not inside you! It does not touch you!

- Argue not. The elephant does not want to be convinced of its irrationality. It wants to rejoice in it. Let it do what it must—to express its elephant nature in the only way it can under the circumstances: by being angry. Exist in the nimbus of the elephant's rage. Do Nothing. Under no circumstances allow yourself to fall into reflexive groveling. Groveling is for the guilty. Be strong and tall in your innocence!

- Accept false blame falsely. Be not stiff-necked, rational, or full of self. As a flexible reed, you must be willing to accept blame that is not yours if that is what must be done to make the elephant feel better. An apology for that which you did not do is of no value. Then what does it cost you to offer it? Nothing! "So sorry." See? That was easy! And look—is it possible that, slightly aware of its own unfairness, the elephant is slightly less angry after your act of bogus atonement?

- Promise to help. Promises too are easy to make. You may "get to the bottom of it." You may "find the responsible parties." You may "make sure it doesn't happen again." You may do so many things. Or not. A promise is not a brick.

- Stay put. As opposed to the guilty person, you have nothing of which to be ashamed. Have the courage, then, to exist in the maelstrom of the elephant's anger until it subsides. Leaving implies that you have an action to perform elsewhere to mitigate your guilt. You have no need to fear and are therefore perfect in yourself. Wait. Regard the skyline. Empty your head even further, if possible.

BUDDHA BULLET

◐ The elephant's anger is not the end of the world. The end of the world has already happened because there is no world. There is only everything. So the elephant is angry! Who cares?

LEAVING THE ELEPHANT ALONE

We won because we had a good crew and a strong boat
and lots of experience, and the people who didn't have
those have gone to the big regatta in the sky.

*TED TURNER ON WINNING THE 1979 FASTNET RACE
OFF ENGLAND, WHERE FIFTEEN COMPETITORS
WERE KILLED DURING A GALE*

The great elephant does not loiter on the rabbit's path.

ZEN SUTRA

Two truths arise from these thoughts:

1. Sometimes it's impossible not to be so sick of the elephant that one must absent oneself from its presence. Ted Turner won his boat race because others died in the pursuit of the finish line. The lack of any empathy for those who perished is stunning. One may be excused if one does not wish to remain around the elephant after it expels such a statement, one that reveals the true depth of its coldness, selfishness, and spiritual neutrality.

2. You are a rabbit to the elephant. It has no interest in your path. It is therefore quite easy to get out of the elephant's way for a time and stay there by simply adhering to your own path.

Places to go when you want to go away from the elephant:

- Your office
- A walk
- Lunch
- Minneapolis
- St. Paul
- Los Angeles (when It is in New York)
- New York (when It is in Los Angeles)
- Vegas (for a convention)
- Home
- Rome
- Nome

Reasons to give the elephant for going away from it:

- "I have to go now."
- "See you later."
- "Gee. Look at the time."
- "I'll get back to you on that in a day or two."
- "I'll be in Minneapolis for the rest of the week on that Studtz thing."

BUDDHA BULLETS

◇ Somewhere inside, the elephant knows it is intolerable. You are now advanced enough to dare subtly conveying that message and receiving some respect in return.

◇ It is not bad for the elephant to miss you.

FRIGHTENING THE ELEPHANT WITH MICE

Whatchu talkin' 'bout, Willis?

GARY COLEMAN

Elephants may be made as confused as the rest of us, perhaps even more so, because they believe themselves to be wise and all-knowing. In that ability to create confusion lies the coincident ability to control that which you have made confused.

The masters tell a story. One day a great nabob and warrior came to see the Buddha. The Buddha was quite busy but squeezed in a couple of minutes to see the celebrity business honcho anyway. The nabob was well-known and wealthy, but looking upon the strength and serenity of the Buddha and the simplicity of his surroundings, he was suddenly struck by a wave of insecurity, the feeling that lurks behind the bold front of many a powerful and rich potentate.

He said to Buddha, "What's up with this? I'm a big deal. Everybody does what I say and I could go out right now and buy a car with the money in my pocket. But looking at you, I'm nervous and full of self-doubt. What's going on here?"

"Wait until I'm done with the rest of my business, and I'll fill you in," the Buddha said.

The rest of the day, the Buddha took calls, had a long working lunch in the conference room, and met with dozens of people in a succession of short meetings where a lot got done with little fanfare. Throughout this normal succession of events, the big mogul waited.

Finally, at the end of the day, the Buddha said, "Okay, come with me." He walked his visitor to the elevator bank and pressed the button. "You see," said the Buddha, "I made you so nervous I was able to keep you waiting rudely all day with no particular promise of giving you anything. You see how easy it is to put a shoe on the other foot. Now get out of here."

And the mogul went away, amazed, somewhat enlightened, and relieved.

Those who do not understand the importance of this story are instructed to read it again and again until either:

1 You understand it, or
2 You give up and go on to the next chapter.

Here is some assistance for the unraveling of this koan: Elephants are not afraid of big things or are at least unwilling to admit to such fear either to themselves or others. They are elephants!

Elephants are therefore left only the option of being afraid of little things that sneak up and surprise them. Such things include mice, loud noises, spreadsheet surprises and sudden disappointments, food that is on the menu but unavailable, unannounced visitors, word of the displeasure of a higher executive, bad news about the effect of NutraSweet on the human kidney.

◆ There are so many tiny things that can go wrong and upset the elephant's equilibrium!

◆ Big creatures need equilibrium to remain viable. The slightest push of the right kind can send them toppling.

◆ You can provide destabilizing small matters quite easily . . .

◆ . . . and thereby accomplish the ultimate goal of the intermediate elephant handler: to at once create a problem and provide its immediate solution.

It's like telling Mozart that there are too many notes in an
opera. Which one do you want us to take out?

*GORDON M. BETHUNE, CHAIRMAN OF CONTINENTAL
AIRLINES, RESPONDING TO GOVERNMENT CRITICISM THAT
CARRIERS SCHEDULE TOO MANY FLIGHTS*

I stuck my finger in Sandy's eye.

*JAMIE DIMON ON CRITICIZING HIS FORMER BOSS
AND MENTOR SANDY WEILL*

Elephants believe they can accept criticism. In this, as in
so many things, they delude themselves.

True, it is possible that Jamie Dimon's firing at the
hands of his corporate Moses had nothing to do with
the protégé having achieved a level of importance at
which he felt comfortable sticking his finger in the elephant's eye. It is also possible that pigs have wings.

Any bitter pill of criticism one offers an elephant
must be buried within a vast tub of cream cheese. As it is
written:

Proportion of Praise to Criticism in Healthy Elephant/Handler Relationship

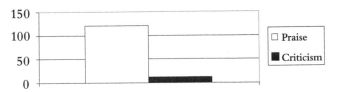

There are, of course, many ways to offer the praise that must always come before the dangerous alternative:

* Directly
* Obliquely
* From beneath
* In small, tasty packets
* Dragging in a large bale of it and depositing it directly at the elephant's feet
* In public, with ceremony
* In private, as a gift
* Loud
* Soft
* You get the idea! Invent your own!

There are, however, exactly five ways to offer small, careful criticisms when it is absolutely necessary. Here they are:

1 In private, as the barest wisp of the possibility of a minor sublikelihood that something might perhaps have been done amiss.

2 In public, as a loud and direct criticism of another person. "I can't believe you did this, Morty," you might

say to Morty, if such be his name. Morty then has two choices. He may defend himself or, more likely, agree with you about the offending thing. Or he may turn to the elephant and say, "Actually, it wasn't me who did that. It was the elephant here." Naturally, no one would choose the latter course of action, so your criticism is essentially safe if offered in such a way that the elephant does not feel the need to rear up on its haunches and slap you down.

3 The honest E-mail. It may begin, "I have been thinking about YOUR ISSUE HERE, Mark, and I still can't wrap my mind around your assumptions. Let me offer some others." This is businesslike and involves no loss of elephant face. Elephants are fond of their faces and will appreciate your efforts to join them in preserving theirs.

4 Get someone else to do it. Choose someone who will not fall to his or her knees screaming, "Bob made me do it!"

5 The long face. A picture is worth a thousand words! Make yourself a picture of misery. The elephant may get the hint.

BUDDHA BULLETS

◆ The road is littered with the bodies of those who believed that elephants love to hear the truth, even when it is detrimental to their self-image.

◆ The gods hate gratuitously stupid people who bring destruction down upon themselves. That includes Buddhist gods as well as other kinds.

◆ Consider forgetting about it, why don't you?

FIGHTING WITH THE ELEPHANT

Either I get Frank's job as president, or I'm going to leave
the company.

*JEFFREY KATZENBERG TO DISNEY CHAIRMAN MICHAEL EISNER
LESS THEN THIRTY-SIX HOURS AFTER THE DEATH OF DISNEY
NUMBER TWO, FRANK WELLS*

I hate the little midget.

MICHAEL EISNER ON JEFFREY KATZENBERG

Martial arts are a part of Zen. As Sensei Chuck Norris
has observed, "True martial artists, when teaching or
training, realize that every move they make is a philosophy not of violence, but of life." That is, when all else
fails and one must fight, the battle must be viewed as a
path to creation, not destruction.

Of course this is the most dangerous activity in
which a budding bodhisattva can indulge. Even if you
are not expunged immediately, elephants have a well-
known capacity for remembering battles won and lost,
particularly against an adversary upon whose incentive
package they must pass.

As it is written: It is advisable for those who wish to
keep their status, position, and unquestioned expense
account to beat the elephant without it knowing you
have done so.

This may be done in one of two ways: so quickly that the elephant does not know it has been struck until its severed head is flying across the room, or two, so slowly and patiently that the creature has no idea it has been in a fight at all.

FIGHTING THE ELEPHANT: QUICK

- Supreme awareness of the issue about which you are to battle the elephant comes first. Salary? When you may take your vacation? The acquisition of a new laptop? The destruction of a hated adversary for whom the elephant has shown suspicious tolerance? What is the issue? And more important— What . . . do . . . you . . . want?
- That's right. What is your objective? $14,564 in your next year's package? A new BMW? The right to go to the annual retreat in Carefree, Arizona? The elephant's understanding as to why the industry is making it impossible for you to achieve your third-quarter targets? Whatever your actual focus, you are reaching for the heart of the elephant.
- Plant your feet. Not your real feet; the feet upon which your spirit stands. Make sure they are grounded and that your chi is centered over them. Only from that position will you be ready to strike.
- Now! In one alarming, violent action, plunge your hand into the elephant's chest and rip its steaming heart from its moorings. Only if you have the

stomach for this act should you contemplate fighting with the elephant. Aim well. For such a big beast, the elephant's heart is amazingly small.

- Hold on to the elephant's heart until it gives you what you want. Be prepared to articulate what you want. The elephant is not a mind reader.

- Return the elephant's heart to its chest. When it is back in its proper resting place, you may retreat without further comment or remain with the elephant to chat while you both compose yourselves and reestablish your customary footing.

- There is no chance that the elephant will believe that for a time you actually held its central muscle in your hand. It will believe the incident to have been a dream. But it will adhere to its promise. If it does not, it is possible you never successfully extracted its heart at all.

- If the acquisition of the heart does not work—and it should!—it may be necessary for you to go for a different organ. But the elephant's heart is the best and most reliable one for the granting of wishes. Others are messier.

FIGHTING THE ELEPHANT: SLOW

- This is far more dangerous. The elephant will not know it is in a fight, but it will be aware that you are suddenly most annoying in some indefinable way. *Be careful.*

- Focus again on your agenda. General, vague grappling with an elephant can only end one way—

with your career mashed to the consistency of hummus and spread around on the ground for people to step in.

- Get up on your karmic toes—the toes that may elevate your spirit as much as possible without requiring that it leave the ground. Make sure that you are well balanced and that you can leap this way and that with agility and confidence if necessary.

- Now, slowly, slowly . . . so that the elephant has no idea that you have done so . . . creep up upon the beast and grab ahold of its gigantic ear . . . with your teeth. Once you have bit down on the ear, do not let it go until the elephant has granted your wish. This is quite difficult, obviously. If it were easy, you wouldn't be in a fight.

- You must be prepared to speak, eat, and converse with your body while your spirit has its jaws clenched to the elephant's ear. You must also be ready to have your chi whipped back and forth through the air, slammed against trees, and otherwise battered during this long ordeal.

- When the elephant has given you what you want, let go of its ear and by all means leave its presence until its amnesia for unpleasant events sets in. If possible, do not return until the elephant inquires after your presence.

ONE FINAL NOTE

- Never, ever exult in your victory, inform anyone else of your victory, or indicate to anyone at all that a battle has taken place. It has not, indeed. For who could battle an elephant and win? Certainly not you!

BUDDHA BULLET

❖ There is only one other way to best an elephant in battle—to do so as part of a pack of jackals. That method will not be taught here.

FIGHTING SIDE BY SIDE WITH THE ELEPHANT

As relates to the competition, I'm the meanest mother-
fucker on the planet.

THOMAS M. SIEBEL
CHAIRMAN
SIEBEL SYSTEMS

Fighting alongside the elephant is the best fun in the world. Elephants are competitive. They love to battle against any enemy. When you find yourself on the same side as the beast, consider it one of the great luxuries of business life.

Perhaps the only thing better is dying beside the elephant. That is a pleasure that can only be tasted once.

BUDDHA BULLET

○ Stand up. Stand tall. Fight and die. What more do you need to know?

IGNORING THE ELEPHANT
IN SPITE OF HIS SIZE AND WEIGHT

We were a flea attacking an elephant.

SAM WALTON, FOUNDER OF WAL-MART, ON COMPETING WITH KMART

Don't you ever turn your back on me when I'm talking.

CITIGROUP SENIOR EXECUTIVE JAMIE DIMON TO THE COMPANY'S VICE CHAIRMAN, DERYCK MAUGHAN, AT A BLACK-TIE DINNER. WHEN MAUGHAN TURNED AWAY FROM HIM, DIMON GRABBED HIM BY THE SHOULDERS AND SPUN HIM AROUND, POPPING A BUTTON FROM THE LAPEL OF HIS DINNER JACKET

As it is written, and as we have seen, the Buddha began his adult life in a three-piece suit, with a cell phone, Rolodex, and leather Day-Timer. He had a wife and children and took the 6:38 each night back to his suburban domicile. His father played a large role in his life and was well pleased with his son's success.

And then one day the Buddha walked away from all of that, because he saw the central role that suffering played in the life of men and women and sought to eradicate it. He would not have become the Buddha if he had not done so.

Arrayed before him were many elephants, with many elephant needs, but those elephants became as nothing to him, and he ignored their size, their weight, the possibility that they could step on his face. And then, as if by magic, by the simple act of denying the elephants' power over him, they became as nothing, lighter than air, all but invisible.

Free and unencumbered, the man stepped off into the path that would lead to the Bodhi Tree, a very common sort of tree to be found just about anywhere.

The elephants were not happy with the man at all. They raged. They stormed. They canceled his credit cards. But the Buddha was on his own path, and he ignored them once again, and in that ignoring were the seeds of enlightenment and freedom.

It is also written that this ignoring brought with it much pain. The Buddha was forced to dress in odd clothing. You see it in the statues. He didn't have a decent steak for over a decade. He got rained on. He could afford only bad shoes. And he suffered terribly over the acts of social renunciation that had made elephants he loved so unhappy with him.

BUDDHA BULLET

◑ The price of ignoring the elephant is high. But it is an action to which all students must come, at least once in their life. Begin small, by ignoring your elephant over the weekends. See how it goes from there.

SHOWING GRATITUDE TO THE ELEPHANT

If you pick up a starving dog and make him prosperous,
he will not bite you. That is the principal difference
between a dog and a man.

MARK TWAIN

If the elephant has given you heartburn, has it not also
provided the trip to New Orleans that caused it? If it has
given you the propensity to jump six feet in the air when
you hear a twig crack, has it not also provided the back-
yard and chaise lounge in which you sit listening to the
sounds of the forest?

The elephant contributes much to your life. It gives you
subjects other than death to worry about. It gives you the
possibility of greater things to come. It gives you a point
around which to focus your emotions, your dreams both
long- and short-term, your hatred, your love.

It is only right that you show gratitude. It is also good
politics.

There are many actions the elephant may perform
to earn your gratitude. But as the Buddha said when
an elderly retainer gave him three silk ties from
Bergdorf's, "Good things are much appreciated, as
long as they do not wear their agenda like a pimple on
the nose for all to see. There is a big difference between grateful student and a smarmy suckup! It is a

matter of degree. Now take these away. They're not my pattern."

Not that the Buddha was angry, for the Buddha did not get angry. But from that time forth he did have that fellow's number. "Why don't you give me another tie, Bob," the Buddha would ask him periodically. What divine laughter that would produce!

BUDDHA BULLETS

On Gratitude

Elephant . . .	You Give the Elephant . . .
Allows you to keep working	Nothing
Gives you a 5% raise	A short word in the elevator
Gives you a 10% raise	A thank-you note
Gives you a big bonus	A nice birthday gift (less than $200)
Gives you stock options	Your undying loyalty
Gives you a company car	Your firstborn child
Spares you in a headcount cut	A quiet, sincere speech of appreciation late at night when all others have gone home
Is caught with strippers in Vegas	Some form of deniability
Is unjustly fired in big shake-up	A firm handshake

I don't smoke with my prostate.

SOUTHWEST AIRLINES CEO HERBERT KELLEHER EXPLAINING WHY HE CONTINUES TO CHAIN-SMOKE EVEN THOUGH HE HAS BEEN DIAGNOSED WITH PROSTATE CANCER

Elephants, like children, believe they are indestructible. And like children, they are vulnerable, ungainly, naked, and hairless beasts, altogether susceptible to the wind, rain, and snow, not to mention the assaults of other elephants, jackals, and even people.

Unfortunately, the elephant does not appreciate your attempt to protect it. Believing in its own perfection and invulnerability, it will likely be annoyed if it sees you attempting to buffer it from harm. It is an elephant, after all, and therefore impervious to destruction!

Several years ago, the Buddha found himself sojourning with a medium-size elephant that was extremely good of heart but subject to significant self-delusion.

This nice but slightly deluded elephant had a past career in the military and believed that creatures in the same organization were programmed to be loyal to each other. In this regard he was for the most part correct, except that he included senior management in this worldview. Wrong. The Buddha saw that the elephant believed in the essential loyalty of his boss elephants, and his heart grieved.

And when the time came to decide who was going to run this elephant's corner of the world after a significant merger, he went to see the head elephant, who was not only his boss but, as the smaller elephant firmly believed, his friend.

"You are my elephant," said the older and larger of the two elephants. "When the whole deal comes down, you're the elephant I want to be at the head of the pack." And the smaller elephant came back to the office all full of hope and beans and told the Buddha, "Murray is my friend and would not lie to me. I am his guy and everything is going to be fine."

The Buddha, breaking from his usual form, told the elephant that he was living in Lala-land. That if the senior elephants had ever wanted to take care of matters the right way, they would already have done so. "Murray is my friend and a great and loyal elephant," said the small and slightly addled elephant. "He would never screw me."

And the Buddha saw that there was nothing he could do to protect the elephant, because it was in the elephant's Elephant Nature to pursue its own destruction: with energy and determination and full confidence in that it was right. After trying to save the elephant from itself without being cruel to the elephant, the Buddha sat back and did what is most proper for Buddhas to do: nothing.

You can do nothing to protect the elephant from its Elephant Nature. But you can try. Trying and Doing Nothing are not incompatible. In the Trying, there is Duty. In the Doing Nothing, there is the peace that comes with Zen.

Do both at once.

You may attempt to protect the elephant from things that might hurt it. But all such Trying must masquerade as general competent service of the elephant, not as protection against discomfort or physical injury. The elephant does not want to be protected.

To do the job right, you must have the proper defensive tools, and you must know how to whirl them over your head like the sword of the dedicated samurai. Die, elephant enemies!

BUDDHA BULLETS

ELEPHANT DEFENSE TOOLS

◇ *THE TOWN CAR:* It protects the elephant from the elements and other people who might intrude on its hermetically sealed existence. The seal is good. Try to maintain it. Elephants are rarely hurt inside the seal.

◇ *THE SCHEDULING BOOK:* If you can control the contents of the elephant's interfaces, you can do much to keep it from harm's way. The current president of the United States, for instance, is nicely managed by his handlers and eats little that is not prechewed by professionals.

This makes him a much more effective elephant than he would have been in an unprotected environment, and more capable of running free when he needs to.

◆ **THE TRUTH:** If the elephant decides to paint all of the fall inventory red because it had a dream instructing it to do so, it may be necessary for the elephant to hear a few things. Telling the Truth is the way of Zen. Getting killed for it, however, is not.

◆ **DOING NOTHING:** When the inevitable happens, the elephant will need a kind, loving, and dispassionate caretaker to help it to its feet and pour alcohol on its wounds. This is not easy. On the bright side, the alcohol is often free.

> When the elephants fight, the grass gets trampled.
>
> *AFRICAN PROVERB*

So don't be lying in the grass, fool. Stand up. Look about you. And vamoose.

Of course, it may not be quite that simple. There is, as always, room for meditation to provide insight and strategy before one cuts and runs.

First, evaluate. Is this indeed a collision? If you are doing well, you are often in rooms with more than one large beast. If they are elephants worthy of the name, they will constantly be testing each other, poking each other for soft spots, trying to see whose tusks are longer. This is to be expected and must not disquiet you.

Anybody but a total lunkhead, however, can spot thunderheads when they are building in the sky.

We have read and thought deeply about the titanic struggle between Citigroup coexecutive pachyderms Sandy Weill and John Reed. In the days leading up to their final encounter, they would often find themselves in planning meetings of some vague sort or another. One day, according to the Kama Sutra of capital (the *Wall Street Journal*), Mr. Weill asked Mr.

Reed a business question. As Mr. Reed answered, Mr. Weill made a show of publicly rolling his eyes. A few moments later, when Mr. Weill began to speak, Mr. Reed made sure that those present could see that he had just found something of overpowering interest to read. To anyone in the room, it was clear where matters stood, and the safest place to stand was clearly not in that room.

There are several ways to see if two powerful elephants in your purview are preparing to collide:

- Your elephant refers to the other as Fartface.
- You are invited to attend a meeting with the other elephant, and your elephant finds out about it. For two days he sticks the end of his tusk into your rear end until sitting down in any seat, no matter how soft, is a total misery.
- Your elephant complains to you directly about the other. You are then required to add your outraged voice to that of the elephant. Woe to you if you do not!

Next, determine which elephant will win. If you look with your Zen eye, it should be obvious. Which of the two looks like it could eat two pounds of raw meat without twitching off a fly? Which of the two looks nervous and restive?

Survival is a necessary part of service, too. So when the minimum is accomplished, the smart intermediate handler gets gone. Regret not this seeming cowardice. Elephants can take care of themselves, and sometimes they should have to.

❍ The dead know glory. But they do not enjoy it.

When the Elephant Has Gone off You for a While

I can go from being hysterical . . . to being over it five
minutes later. If I didn't emote, it would be impossible to
do my job.

Mary Meeker
Morgan Stanley's top Internet analyst

All created things will pass away. When one achieves the
wisdom to realize this, one may rise above this world of
sorrow.

The Dhammapada

Women and elephants never forget an injury.

Saki

There is a great lie told about elephants, one that is generally believed by people who have not known them: an
elephant never forgets.

Like all great lies, there is some truth in it. Only a
slight modification renders it completely accurate: an
elephant never forgets an indignity.

Kindness, friendship, and even love, however, are
easily erased from the elephant mind. This is because all
elephants suffer from emotional amnesia. This ailment, if
such it be, grows more acute as the elephant gets bigger.

But in truth, it is not a liability, for its emotional amnesia enables the beast to travel with a light trunk.

Here is how it works:

Arc of Emotional Memory over Time

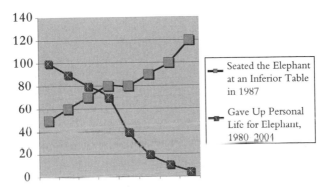

That is, the elephant's memory of things and people that hurt its pride grows over time. The reporter who made fun in print of the elephant's tie may, ten years later, be abused at a party. The loyal employee who slept weeks on end in seedy motels, canvassing the nation for the benefit of the elephant's bottom line, is easily dispatched in the latest headcount cut with no loss of sleep for the elephant. For that, as we know, is business.

One time, it is written, the Buddha was sojourning with a mighty elephant who had only recently come into his full power. This beast was then enjoying the first flush of its newfound success. "I received a call yesterday," the elephant told the Buddha, stating that the call was from possibly the only bigger elephant in the forest.

"What did he want?" asked the Buddha.

"He said, 'Hey, now that you're a huge elephant, I thought we should probably have lunch,' " said the elephant with a smile.

"And what did you say?" said the Buddha with that small anticipatory smile of his.

"I said, 'No thanks. You didn't answer my phone calls before, why should you want to have lunch with me now?' " And then the elephant laughed. And so did the Buddha. And then they had coffee.

You see? An elephant never forgets an indignity—anything that hurt its feelings, which, while it has little consideration for those of others, are very, very tender indeed. Do not, therefore, hurt the elephant's feelings, or you may be forced to start over again with a brand-new elephant.

Things, however, the elephant does forget:

- Things you have done to make it happy.
- Things you have done to make it sad.
- Things you have done to make it angry.
- Things you have done.
- You.

This is excellent news indeed for those who serve, handle, fondle, wheedle, cajole, lead, and otherwise manipulate the elephant.

Certainly, the elephant seems to hate you now and then. But lacking any reason—small or large, silly or serious, real or imagined—such animosity from the great gray beast means nothing at all.

Take this thought on the tip of your tongue. Taste it, savor it. Mmmmmm. Is that not good?

The elephant does not like you today . . . ?

And . . . who cares! What a mountain of joy lies hidden in the cloud of uncaring that is the practice of Business Zen!

◇ Here is a list of things that, while they may make a great deal of difference to the lives of others, should mean nothing to you personally because you did not cause them and cannot affect them:

  ✓ Earthquakes
  ✓ Water shortages
  ✓ Weather
  ✓ They're out of pecan pie
  ✓ Massive layoffs caused by mergers
  ✓ Sudden deaths about which people say, "Wow, he just keeled over in the elevator!" (including yours)
  ✓ The elephant decides it's mad at you and/or takes out some passing mood on you

◇ If, on the other hand, you enjoy being a schmuck and beating yourself over the head for things you didn't do simply because an authority figure decides to play with your head, go ahead. But that has nothing to do with either Duty or Buddha. Go directly to the Self-Help shelf at your local bookseller's and pick up something on self-esteem.

◇ If your elephant has you in the doghouse, keep working, stay out of its sight, and let the river flow. Why not go visit another elephant for a while and see what other people have to deal with. The grass is always grayer on the other side of the reporting structure.

When the Elephant Seems to Have Gone off You for Good

I never saw it coming. I thought one day we'd have a
drink and work it out.

JAMIE DIMON, ABOUT BEING FIRED BY HIS MENTOR SANDY
WEILL

There is no shark like hatred.

BUDDHA, QUOTED IN THE FORBES SCRAPBOOK OF THOUGHTS
ON BUSINESS LIFE

There is a difference between passing cruelty, incon-
stancy, rudeness, and neglect (that is, business as
usual) . . . and the determination to get rid of you. Not
because it is angry with you . . . but simply because it
has decided that its world would be a better place without you.

The peace and wisdom gained in the previous chapter should allow you to see that difference. If you do not
start at every shadow, if you do not tremble at every
stamp of the elephant's foot, you will not know when
the true scythe of death has come to call.

This has nothing to do with anger, and everything to
do with regret. It is the end of your time as handler of
this elephant, unless you take certain dramatic steps.

Jamie Dimon thought that he and the Weillephant
would one day share a drink and work it out? In his

dreams! The big one was done with his former protégé and couldn't wait to enjoy the future without him. Why? Because suddenly, it could.

As great as is the elephant's love when it exists, so grand and sweeping is its capacity to flush that love from its system when it is over. Such it is with the beasts we serve.

Indeed, an elephant who is finished with you will wipe you out with neither pleasure nor displeasure, no matter how much history you share, because at the heart of the elephant, there is no heart. There is only business. And the elephant likes it that way.

"He's a good guy," the elephant will say to its fellow grayskins. "But he had to go. It's not personal. It's business."

And so it is.

Why, then, does it feel so personal to us? Because we are foolish and benighted and live in utter darkness.

And yet it need not be so. We can be as cold and businesslike as elephants, if we embrace the teaching of Not-Caring that is central to our practice. This is particularly true when we come to the point when we realize that the elephant on whom we depend would like to eliminate us from its view. All seems lost. But there is still one thing that may be done. It is difficult . . . but it may be done.

Prepare yourself. You have come to the Moment of Submission.

Think of it thus: You are a candy bar. Nothing can take away your sweet, chewy center. The outer layers, however, must be molded to fit the elephant's needs, perhaps for one last time.

There is great freedom in being that which you are not. True slavery lies only in bondage to oneself. That is why, as difficult as service is . . . total submission is far harder. It is, however, what is necessary for you now. It is a new face you must put on—one you have never before worn.

Fortunately, we have for guidance in this difficult task the words of the Buddha himself, in a possibly apocryphal sutra passed down by students who hung with the master one long weekend while a difficult merger was being worked out. For some reason these deals always happen around Labor Day, possibly because senior elephants get lonely around that time, and the group was condemned to pass untold hours in a rural Sheraton Centre waiting for bean counters to whip up the next round of projections.

During that time, the group of younger acolytes approached the Buddha and asked how it was possible to keep their jobs when it was clear that their elephant had slated them for destruction in the upcoming deal. Here is a record of that discussion.

Q: Buddha, are you busy?

A: What is busy? I'm sort of busy all the time, but for some things I am never busy.

Q: We are here because we are convinced that our senior managers have grown tired of us and are now determined to trade us in for newer models.

A: Did you screw up in some way?

Q: Possibly. None of us is particularly brilliant. We are simply average people doing as good a job as possible.

A: Have you offended your master in any specific way?

Q: Possibly. We can be annoying at times.

A: Your master is no longer speaking with you?

Q: Not unless spoken to.

A: Ah. Then a positive act of submission to your elephant is required. You must lie down in front of the beast, place its foot upon your head, and beg it to do its will. Only in this way will the elephant's sense of balance be challenged, and its determination to destroy you be allayed.

Q: This is a most disturbing course of action, Master.

A: Yes, it is. Few are strong enough to offer complete submission. Most cling to false strength and unwarranted pride and are therefore crushed under the weight of the inevitable.

Q: When is the Moment of Submission?

A: Neither too soon nor too late. Let me tell you a story.

Q: Oh, good.

A: A young friend of mine was named to an executive position not long ago. He was smart and talented and very hardworking, but no more a genius than anyone else. About six months into his new assignment, a senior elephant returned from a long trip to the Far East and parked itself in the office down the hall from my young friend.

Almost immediately, it became clear that the new elephant was going to sit on my young friend and all but do his job for him. There was much friction and everybody was unhappy.

"What shall I do, Buddha?" the young man asked me. And I answered him thusly: "Which would you rather keep? Your high position or your pride?" And it was so. He would submit. Or he would be gone. "Go," I told him. "Make it possible for this elephant to view you as an acolyte, not an enemy. Feign love. Pretend loyalty. Do what you are told. Break your pride in half, fold it neatly, and stick it in your ear."

This is what the young man did, my friends. Today, he is a powerful deputy to that great elephant and most clearly the heir apparent to a large and lucrative turf.

He neither anticipated the elephant's displeasure, becoming a toady when such was not warranted, nor waited until the elephant was enraged and incapable of viewing the young man as a usable object. He played it perfectly, and his pride, once abandoned, has replanted itself and flowered like one of those gigantic sunflowers one often sees along the highway in the Midwest.

Q: Thank you, Buddha.
A: Don't mention it.

BUDDHA BULLETS

◌ The elephant is capable of hatred and meanness as large as its appetite. It is a business machine.

◌ The elephant must view you as an extension of its needs and desires. If you are very good, it will convince itself that it has a fondness for you and will desire to preserve you, at least for a time.

◆ Most often, you can serve simply by accomplishing Duty. At times, however, normal Duty will not serve. Submission then becomes the considered course.

◆ Don't do it if you don't want to. It is an extremely painful process, and as we have seen, nothing makes any difference anyway.

◆ On the other hand, if nothing makes any difference, why not try?

The wise who control their body, who likewise control
their speech, the wise who control their mind are indeed
well controlled.

THE DHAMMAPADA

We have seen the bottomless well of satisfaction that
comes with the end of striving, the end of wanting, the
end of emotion.

We have seen that, unlike you, the great elephants
do not concern themselves with personal feelings,
because they have taught themselves to view the vast
range of human interactions as "just business," nothing
more, and that this distance gives them incalculable
power.

> *Tom tosses people out left and right on a whim. He's a
> vindictive, ruthless guy. Most people play by win/win
> rules. He plays win/lose—he wants to crush you.*
>
> FORMER SIEBEL EMPLOYEE

Love too has power and can be an excellent weapon,
but only if one is the thing that is loved, not the lover.
Sadly, most often the elephant is the object that is loved.

It is almost impossible to serve one without, at some point, coming to project all sorts of affection upon the unworthy beast. One finds its habits cute, after a time. One forgives its unkindnesses and indulges its peccadilloes. One needs to love the thing one serves. That is the great weakness of the untutored, un-Zen mind.

Sadly, the elephant is a most untrustworthy repository for such exalted emotional gifts. Too often, it returns that honor with dust and ashes.

Therefore, do not love, if you can help it. Or if you do love, recognize that love for what it is—a weakness born of the intensity of the stakes, the proximity and the experience of service. And never presume that your love is returned in the same spirit in which it is given. You will be disappointed.

> *I hope the worms eat his eyes out.*
> JIMMY HOFFA, ON HEARING OF PRESIDENT JOHN F. KENNEDY'S ASSASSINATION

Hatred is also a bad strategy. It is an acid that ultimately destroys the one who hates and rarely touches the thing that is hated. Jimmy Hoffa, for instance, was a big hater. Was that capacity for hating somehow related to the karma that eventually deposited Mr. Hoffa under the cement in the end zone at Giants Stadium? You decide.

As it is written in the *Mahabharata*: "The person who looks upon others as he looks upon himself, who has given up retaliation, who has conquered anger, obtains happiness in the next world."

And perhaps even this one.

Alternatives to Love and Hatred

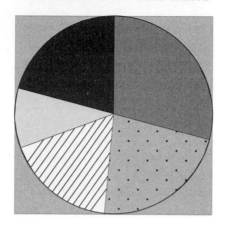

■ Indifference ▦ Attention to Duty □ Social Relations
▨ Model Trains ■ Food and Drink

BUDDHA BULLETS

○ Rent the movie *Old Yeller*.

○ Watch it with several small children.

○ When you are capable of viewing, without weeping, the part where the dog dies, you are getting there.

○ When the part where the dog dies makes you want to laugh, you are ready for the next plateau.

Exchanging Your Old Elephant for a New One

You're not the boss of me now,
And you're not so big.

THEY MIGHT BE GIANTS

Et tu, Brute? Then fall, Caesar!

JULIUS CAESAR, UPON THE LOSS OF HIS KEY LIEUTENANT

There are a lot of elephants in the world. There is yours. There is Brewster's. Yours is, of course, the greatest. But then there are all the others.

Keep your eyes open. A time may come when you must apply your efforts to a new creature entirely. This will be clear because your elephant is either dying or already dead.

One may tell that an elephant is dying because it smells even worse than usual and is being avoided by all other elephants. In the final stages, the elephant may become quite vicious and attempt to strike out at its enemies, using you as a weapon. It is inadvisable to be that weapon.

It is also possible for a dying elephant to lie down right on top of you when it is looking for its final resting place. Obviously, this is not a healthy place to be.

◌ It is possible to go shopping for a new elephant when yours is no longer viable, but it is better to hold yourself in a position of receptivity and availability.

◌ Show no public regret for your dying elephant, or people will feel inclined to bury you with it.

◌ Show no public censure for your dying elephant, either. Elephants hate disloyal handlers and will not attach themselves to you if they feel you might not mourn their passing when it is their time for the graveyard.

◌ If you have fought your best and your elephant is indeed doomed, take ten steps away from the dying beast and stay there. In a while, something will happen to you independent of the fate of the elephant.

◌ Above all, avoid the temptation to indulge in non-Zen paroxysms of guilt. If you were to go, the elephant might feel some regret, it is true. But it would not miss a meal, would it?

I have no talent; I make Ready Wit my Talent.

I have no friends; I make my Mind my Friend.

I have no enemy; I make Incautiousness my Enemy.

I have no armor; I make Benevolence my Armor.

I have no castle; I make Immovable Mind my Castle.

I have no sword; I make No Mind my Sword.

SAMURAI CREED
JUCU DOJO WEB PAGE

SOME PREFATORY REMARKS

> The reasonable man adapts himself to the world; the unreasonable one persists in trying to adapt the world to himself. Therefore all progress depends on the unreasonable man.
>
> *GEORGE BERNARD SHAW*

We have spent much time getting to know our beast. We have drunk with it, taken meals with it, told it what it wants to hear and even, as we progressed, what it doesn't.

We have endured its anger, survived even its intention to be rid of us at times. We have learned to care nothing about its noise and smell, to care nothing about anything, because indeed there is no anything, there is only nothing, and within that nothing, Duty.

The final lesson now lies within our grasp. Or rather, within our Mind's grasp.

With that Mind, we may now take hold of the elephant and strip it of its one remaining unmanageable mystery: its weight.

How can this be done? By employing the same practice we have used until this moment. We will breathe. We will meditate. We will keep our sweet and empty center. We will keep our spirit eye on the great totality of the universe, within which both we and the elephant are but meaningless specks. In the great burning furnace, does it matter which of two insignificant morsels of ash is slightly greater in size as each rises slowly to become one with the sky?

It is nugatory.

Throwing an elephant takes courage, but not thought. The moment we stop and consider what we are doing, what we are attempting to accomplish, the elephant will reappear as its corporeal self—and fall to earth.

Who in his right mind would consider throwing an elephant? No one. But we are not in our right mind, are we. We have chosen instead to be in our Right Mind. And that will make all the difference.

GETTING A LEASH ON THE ELEPHANT

With the energy of his whole being, the boy has at last
taken hold of the ox:
But how wild his will, how ungovernable his power!
At times he struts up a plateau,
When lo! He is lost again in a misty, impenetrable moun-
tain pass.

THE TEN OXHERDING PICTURES

First we must get a leash onto the elephant. What is this leash? Is it made of leather? Certainly not.

No, the leash of which we speak is the leash of the elephant's attention. As much control as you have exerted up to this point, the elephant will persist in wandering away whenever its intensely active brain decides to focus on something other than you for a while.

You cannot throw an elephant whose attention is focused elsewhere.

The leash is the bond of attention that exists between you and your elephant. It must be woven from the fabric of your patience and concentration, then hung loosely around the beast's neck.

It is written that a Zen master of some youth but considerable experience worked closely with one extremely elderly elephant who had achieved much in his life span and still had some juice left in him.

The Zen master needed much from the elephant, but the elephant would wander all over the map and insisted, without really thinking about it, in telling the same long, extremely boring stories not twice, not thrice, but every single time anyone attempted to do business with the elephant.

A handler filled with self and the affairs of the day would certainly have either gone completely mad, pointed something out to the elephant about this annoying habit, or simply jumped to the business matters that were his urgent focus. But this master had triumphed over self and knew that time was immaterial to him or her who understands the massive insignificance of everything.

So when the elephant said, "Did I tell you about how the prime minister of France asked my opinion about international currency?" the Zen master said no, because he knew that the elephant could not get to Points B through Z without going through Point A.

Thus did the Zen master always retain and hold the attention of his attention-deficit elephant, by patiently understanding the nature of this particular elephant and leading him gently by the leash of the master's own Enlightenment to the work that needed to be done.

BUDDHA BULLETS

❖ Here are the types of elephants that may not be thrown, due to the flimsiness of their leash of attention:

✓ Drunken elephants
✓ Angry elephants

- ✓ Very tired elephants
- ✓ Elephants on the telephone, BlackBerry, or Palm
- ✓ Horny elephants
- ✓ Sleeping elephants
- ✓ Elephants forced to eat salad when they really wanted a big slab of sirloin

◇ Here are the types of elephants that may be thrown with greater ease, due to the potential durability of their leash of attention:

- ✓ Bored elephants
- ✓ Paranoid elephants
- ✓ Lonely elephants
- ✓ Pleasantly sleepy elephants
- ✓ Elephants in a benevolent mood
- ✓ Elephants craving business action (mergers, acquisitions, divestitures, international expansion, etc.; projects that transcend the oppressive tedium of everyday operations)
- ✓ Elephants eating a sirloin

LEADING THE ELEPHANT

If a man were to conquer in a battle a thousand times a
thousand men, and another conquer one himself, he
indeed is the greatest of conquerers.

THE DHAMMAPADA

Skillful pilots gain their reputation from storms
and tempests.

EPICURUS

You now have the elephant in tow. Its natural
predilection will be to pull against the rope, to pursue
its inherent tendency to wander and go where it wishes
to go.

This is exactly what you must allow it to do. One
may not immediately grasp the leash and begin to pull
the gigantic beast around as if it were a French poodle.
That way can only lead to painful failure and the eating
of considerable quantities of dust and dirt.

Still, the leash is now there, and the goal of the handler is simple: to keep that leash as tightly stretched as
possible. If one is strong, and the leash of concentration
is well made by an advanced Zen practitioner, this will
function to constrain the elephant's movements within a
circumscribed area.

This is the beginning of true control, moving the elephant, which possesses a variety of choices at any time, from this:

Elephant Pattern of Action (Unguided)

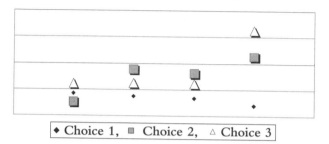

♦ Choice 1, ■ Choice 2, △ Choice 3

To this:

Elephant Pattern of Action (Leashed and Guided)

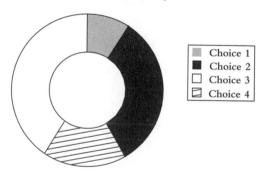

Choice 1
Choice 2
Choice 3
Choice 4

With you in the middle.

After a time, the elephant will forget that it is on a leash and stay within the circle because it lies within the area of maximum comfort for it. Thus it will come to expect the loose control of the leash and in some vague way appreciate it. After a time, it will forget altogether that the leash is there. But its effects will remain, with you now holding the power to influence the general direction of the elephant.

Perhaps it would be appropriate to say that again. You are now in a position—very loosely, it is true—to influence where the elephant will go, and what it will do when it gets there.

There is a reason why assistants and secretarial support are the first and best elephant-throwers. These people quite literally decide where the elephant will lay its head. Will it be booked into The Mirage or the Bellagio? Will it be forced to take a commercial red-eye to make the board meeting in Boca or obtain use of the corporate jet, which would allow it to fly the next morning, early? Will the elephant have a chicken sandwich? Will it be at one o'clock? Which appointments can be blown off with comfort? Does his wife need to know where he is all the time? Think of all the leashes the executive assistant holds in his or her hands!

BUDDHA BULLETS

- You've got the power to lead the beast around by its neck every now and then, and you're getting better all the time.

- Practice! On small items at first, then larger, but only when you are sure of what you want.

- If you are not sure what you want of the elephant at any time, do not bother to lead it. Be content simply to hold the leash.

- But you will never master the ability to throw the elephant by just standing around with a leash in your hands.

- Power must be used, or it is lost.

Mounting the Elephant

True victory is not defeating an enemy. True victory gives
love and changes the enemy's heart.

MORIHEI UESHIBA

You have leashed. You have led. But leading is a slow
process, and very inexact. To drive the elephant where
you truly want it to go, someplace really worth going,
you must get on top of the animal and dig in your
heels.

Once again, you may use the leash of the elephant's
attention as a tool, both during the mounting of the elephant and later, when you need to steer.

Before guidance can begin, you're going to need to
get up there, higher than you've ever been before. You
could, like a tick or a worm, climb laboriously up the
elephant's leg, inching up to your objective one grueling
footstep at a time, digging your boots into its sides,
grasping for purchase in the tender corners of its flesh.

This is a most ignoble route and involves unacceptable
intimacy with the body of the elephant. It is better, and
more fitting with the thoughtless arc of your Enlightenment, to climb upon a neatly piled group of objects
from which you can vault yourself onto the elephant's
back.

What can be used to construct a sturdy pile suitable

for climbing? Golf clubs, furniture, and even paper have been called into service by those in search of a proper medium. But for this purpose, the masters know that nothing serves the function quite so well as other people.

One or two will not do. If you're going to climb over other people to mount your elephant, you're going to need quite a few to get the job done. Getting a mound of people upon which you can get a good footing is difficult and takes time. You have to choose them well and make sure they are completely incapacitated when they are laid end to end and placed in the stack.

You may draw your raw material from two kinds of people:

1 Willing
2 Unwilling

The willing are those who support you every day and would gladly lie down in a nice pile to help you obtain the proper positioning. They include your support staff, anyone else who works for you, clients and vendors whose life you help make possible, peers who may need you to perform a similar service when the time comes for them to toss their leash where it can do the most good.

The unwilling are those whom you may knock briskly over the head to feed the pile you require to get on top of the elephant. They may include the elephant's crusty support staff, peers whose power you can supersede, enemies who can be bullied and manipulated into shape, and possibly the elephant's closest, handpicked cadre of slightly smaller elephants that help it negotiate the hardships of the world.

Willing or unwilling, these are the objects you will need to assemble into a stack that reaches approximately up to the tip of the elephant's ear. When you have done so, grab on to the leash with both hands, take a running start over your pile of allies and tools, and launch yourself at a point on the elephant's back just below the broadest part of the imaginary saddle in its center. When you hit, keep running up the side of the elephant until you find yourself at your goal.

How does it look from up there? A little scary, but good, right?

BUDDHA BULLET

◇ Once you're up there, don't forget to dismiss the group of helpful individuals who helped you mount the elephant. You may need them again!

RIDING THE ELEPHANT

You can teach an elephant to dance, but the likelihood of
its stepping on your toes is very high.

GARY MOSS
VP, CAMPBELL'S SOUP

This is true. But not if you are far above those dangerous
feet. This is the position you have now achieved. If you
had a self, you could now be justifiably proud of it.

As it is, sitting as you now are atop one of the most
fearsome, large, and self-willed beasts in creation, you
may allow yourself to feel some joy—mingled with a
proper appreciation of the associated risks.

You are light, and if you are a good rider, your presence is not annoying to the elephant. Indeed, the elephant finds the control you are exerting pleasurable,
since elephants are themselves grieved, as a rule, by their
unfocused, energetic, and passionate natures. They are
filled with desire and therefore suffer. You are not and
may impart the joy of selfless action to them as you ride
about, invisible to them but in such a way to make them
feel the harmoniousness of existence.

The key, still, is to keep the leash of the elephant's
attention tight in your hand, and to know without ques-

tion where you want the elephant to go. In that regard, it goes without saying that it is far easier to ride the elephant to a clear and focused destination that has some merit in it than to one that is shrouded in uncertainty, mist, and self-aggrandizement.

Good Places to Ride To	Bad Places to Ride To
The location of the next management retreat	Vegas
What to have for lunch	Give you a huge promotion immediately, with lots of money and a new reporting structure
Moving the third-quarter number one percentage point down, given the economy	Change investment banks to one run by your wife's brother
Coming to the right conclusion about Murphy, who is a real jerk	That girl named Heather that he keeps asking about
Not calling a "think tank" meeting over Labor Day weekend because it is lonely and has nothing to do at times when other people are with those they love	Hire a high-profile consulting firm to oversee the reorganization of senior management
Pursuing the kind of acquisitions that build the strength of the company and your management team	Acquire IBM, even though your company now makes the little brushes at the end of vacuum cleaner extensions
Avoiding the urge to bail on the whole thing, sell the company, and leave you and all your pals high and dry	Stop yelling at people because "it's not nice."
Taking you with it to Davos this year	Adopting you as its child

The bigger and more obviously self-serving the destination may be, the worse a rider you will become, as the elephant becomes aware that its desires, which are strong, are not being satisfied by the directions it is taking. Worse, after a time the elephant will become aware of you on top of it and will shake you off its back like an insignificant bird that has been found pecking too aggressively at its hide.

But to those for whom the course is clear and the right object is in view, what greater pleasure can there be than the feeling of riding the beast whose power is now flowing through their hands?

Look at all those little people down below! Smell the air up there! Life is good!

BUDDHA BULLETS

- You may get down at any point by climbing over the elephant's head and clambering down its trunk. Teach the elephant to tolerate this passage, and in time it will learn to hoist you onto its back itself. Then you will really have it made and scarcely require the help of other people at all.

- Don't be reluctant to invite trusted visitors up to ride with you. Those kinds of friendships last almost forever, even when the elephant itself is gone.

LEVERAGING THE ELEPHANT

> The training of Zen meditation helped in two ways: in the cultivation of selflessness and in the dissolution of the distinctions of life and death. The first aided the samurai in cultivating the attitude of complete submission and loyalty to his master. By realizing the truth of selflessness, the samurai could deny himself completely and live his life solely for his lord. The second enabled him to kill and be killed without complaint or fear.
>
> *CHARLES B. JONES*

Many are satisfied with the plesasures and challenges that come with riding. This is certainly understandable. Riding is difficult, and an excellent life can be built on the attainment and perfection of the art.

By leashing, mounting, and riding the beast, we have now become one with it. As we ride upon its back, we have no relative weight, one to the other. This is good, but it is not the ultimate goal, for we are seeking not simply to control the actions of the elephant, but to hold it in our hands and make it fly where we wish.

To move to the next step on our path, we must use the elephant's weight as the source of power that will make this unlikely action possible. This is done through leverage.

The word has been overused quite a bit in recent years. Deals are leveraged. People are leveraged. A seat in the window at Spago is leveraged. Nothing is immune from leverage. Like all overused concepts, it becomes so commonplace that its actual meaning is obscured.

Leverage is the process by which a relatively insignificant force, exerted upon a massive object, makes that object move. The object moves because it is sitting on a device that makes its weight work to amplify the force put against it. That device is a lever.

Anything can be a lever. A pencil. A proxy statement. A newspaper column filled with aggravating stuff. What counts is the point of contact with the mass that optimizes that force put against it. That point is called the fulcrum. You are the fulcrum.

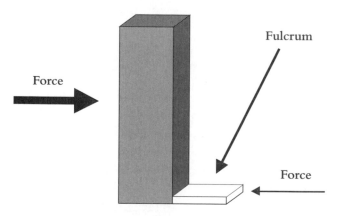

Leverage is why a small samurai can flip a big fat investment banker, or a tiny company with no debt and a little bit of cash can take over a big one. The small entity, placed in exactly the right position, uses the mass and momentum of the larger one to send it in whatever direction the smaller one would like that heavier creature to go.

The bigger the mass and the smaller and more forceful the the act of leverage, the more potential energy that can be generated by the creature to send itself flying. That is the concept. Anyone who doubts its power is referred to the executives at America Online for a lesson. To date, they seem the best at it.

Throwing an elephant is nothing more than the continual application of leverage against its bulk from ever-changing points of opportunity.

Leverage gets the elephant airborne. As it begins to descend, leverage will once again use the elephant's massive momentum to send it aloft.

You must be quick. You must be artful in your application of force. But once off its feet, there is no reason why the elephant should ever touch ground again.

BUDDHA BULLET

◌ Of course it makes no sense. That is why it works.

I think I done seen everything
When I seen an elephant fly.

DUMBO

We have emptied our minds. We have drained our hearts of desire. We have faced the void that lies beneath the veil of existence and followed the path of Duty. In that enlightened and receptive state of thought-free, carefree calm, we have, it is hoped, become proficient in the Zen art of elephant handling.

Consider, for a moment, what we have learned to do to reach this point, where the gigantic elephant lies within our grasp, ready to be thrown.

We have prepared ourselves for the elephant's arrival, met the elephant with Zen precision, greeted it with perfect equanimity. We have learned its language and accepted the responsibility of following along after it with broom and shovel, as was befitting our level of advancement at that time. We have fed the beast the information it needed, watered it with our time and attention. We have polished its tusks and shined its belly with our appreciation, rejoiced with it in victory and consoled it in defeat and disappointment.

Advancing, we have learned to trust the elephant,

knowing that at times it is not worthy of that trust. We have reconciled our intelligence with the duty we bear to obey the beast and developed the subtlety to disobey without consequences.

We have grown ever more sophisticated and adept in our practice, complimenting the elephant in such a way that it comes to crave our admiration, educating the elephant in the matters in which it has no abilities and we have all. As the elephant has become more dependent, we have helped it make up its mind, presenting it with alternative strategies, convincing it that every good idea is its own, garnering some credit when it is due us, shaping the elephant's response to news both good and bad, chatting with it to create affection and a sense of companionship that is not inherent in its nature, drinking with it, laughing with it when nothing is amusing, playing golf with it, enduring its anger when the cause is just, avoiding it when it is not.

We have been through difficult times with our elephant: fighting with it, fighting alongside it, ignoring it when it requires a sense of its own aloneness in the universe or when common sense dictates that we do so. We have done our best to protect it against jackals, kites, lions, and other elephants.

Through it all, we have fought with ourselves, breathing, meditating, reaching deep for the peace and tranquillity that comes with the renunciation of all personal love and hatred, particularly of objects that do not deserve to be repositories of those divine emotions.

Yes, we have worked hard, although we have been sitting. And now we stand alongside a beast that, in spite of its size, weight, and power, is under our control. It does not need us to live its life, unless we have reached a demented level of importance to it. But it does have a strong sense that, in areas of our choosing, it is better to be on our leash than off it.

All that remains is to use the elephant's weight to leverage it again and again into the air in strategic applications of force. The elephant will not fly. It will, however, appear to be flying in a direction of your choosing.

Do not be afraid. If you have succeeded in your practice, the elephant, so big, so strong, so full of food and ideas, means nothing to you. It cannot hurt you. It cannot touch you. You are part of Brahma, and Brahma is around you. There is no move it can make that will turn you around. You are ready.

Position yourself. Select a lever. There are so many. Need you know which to use? Is there not the wealth of the elephant's desires that may be used for your purpose? Its craving for good press? For more money? For sex with gazelles and bunnies? Look about you. Pick up what you need. And apply a short, sharp force, no more than is necessary and no less. The elephant's weight will lean into the blow and look! There it will go.

As the elephant rises into the air, floating like a big gray cloud, take a moment to enjoy the view, the silence about you that you have created. You want nothing. You need nothing. You are nothing. But it is you who have sent the elephant into the air. Isn't that something?

As the beast begins to float back down to earth, select the point from which you will releverage it and send it once more cruising into the ether. Wait. Ah, here it comes.

And there it goes!

◇ There is a big difference between throwing a weight-less object and lifting it. All objects to be lifted have weight. If you are lifting, you have failed. For while throwing an elephant is of course insane and impossible, lifting one can give you an injury requiring immediate attention.

Finding the Elephant in You

We have come to the end of a journey that has no end. And, perhaps, the beginning of another.

Every journey, it is said, begins with a single step. You have taken that step. And without intending to acquire it, you have power. Your Zen practice has, without being designed for that purpose, made you stronger than you ever expected to be. You now have the power that comes of not caring, of not investing emotion into that which does not merit it, of desiring nothing and, as a result, fearing nothing.

What will you do with that power? Will you use it to build on that which you have done and reach for continued, deeper enlightenment? Or will you take the now surprisingly short step toward becoming an elephant yourself? Will you use your power for good, serving the poor beasts who labor under their weight of desire, pain, and self, making their considerable burdens lighter with the excellence of your art?

Or will you turn to the dark side? That way lies

untold agony, continual pain born of the deep well of selfish desire in which the elephant inevitably must fall. And really good food.

We have said from the beginning of this little primer that elephants are born, not made. Although this statement was necessary for your education at the time, it was not completely true.

Stalin sat at the feet of Lenin. Jack Welch was a caddy, as we have seen. George Westinghouse and Thomas Edison were tinkerers, little more. Henry Luce had an idea for a magazine. William Paley thought he might make a living as did his father, selling cigars. Slobodan Milosevic was a party apparatchik. Hitler painted houses. Shakespeare was an actor. Rudolph Giuliani was a federal prosecutor who had more in common with Eliot Ness than Benito Mussolini or, more recently, Winston Churchill. Mao Tse-tung was a schoolteacher. Arnold Schwarzenegger pumped iron. Joan of Arc hung around her hometown church and listened to voices.

For every Gates or Grove who sprang fully formed into their trunk and ears, there are those who made themselves what they became. It is quite possible that you too can use the power you now possess to become one of those colossi who bestride the earth.

Elephant? Or human? You can't be both. The choice is in your hands, little flower. Think about it.

Or better yet, sit down and don't think at all.

Isn't that better?

$(((\text{LISTEN TO})))$

THE COMPLETE WORKS OF STANLEY BING

THROWING THE ELEPHANT

AND

WHAT WOULD MACHIAVELLI DO?

PERFORMED BY
SIMON JONES AND PHILIP BOSCO

The yin and yang of business collected together on 7 CDs!

ISBN 0-06-008559-2 • $29.95 ($44.95 Can.)
7 Hours • 7 CDs • UNABRIDGED
AVAILABLE ONLY ON COMPACT DISC

Available wherever books are sold, or call 1-800-331-3761 to order.

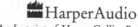

HarperAudio
An Imprint of HarperCollins*Publishers*
www.harperaudio.com